Reviews for *The Future of Real Estate*

T0289437

"It's rare to find someone who is so connected to the real estate industry but is able and willing to assess it objectively, often going against conventional wisdom, popular media, property consultants and property developers. Swee Yong's latest book, like his other books and writings, is highly accessible to the ordinary reader and investor. His views and prognosis are grounded in facts and an impressive grasp of local and global developments and likely trends. His views may not always be welcome but they are needed."

—Dr Mak Yuen Teen
Associate Professor of Accounting, National University of Singapore and Corporate Governance Advocate

"Ku Swee Yong's latest book is a thought-provoking read. The author faces sensitive issues that are relevant to the public head-on and discusses the imminent problems of real estate, including Singapore's aging population, value depreciation of old HDB flats, inevitable job loss under technological disruptions and the massive impact of Covid-19 in different property market segments. He also proposes feasible solutions to these problems, which are strongly supported by relevant facts and figures. Thanks to the author's generous sharing of key data gathered over the years and his own research and analyses of the property landscape, the book debunks myths and provides a glimpse to the future of real estate.

—Vina Ip
Real estate blogger at propertysoul.com

"*The Future of Real Estate* is a provocative, well-researched summary of the challenges and opportunities facing the real estate sector in the next decade and beyond. Swee Yong neatly combines elements of demographics, economics and technology (and more!) into a story that will resonate with Singaporeans of every age and income level. Read it and give a copy to your children so you can prepare for the future together."

—Matthew Dearth
Founder, TRQ Advisors and Adjunct Faculty, Singapore Management University

"This is the first book dedicated to discussing the impact of the Covid-19 pandemic on the property market. Swee Yong is data driven, unafraid to speak his mind and passionate about helping others make informed decisions about huge purchases and investments."

—Jeraldine Phneah
Millennial Blogger, www.jeraldinephneah.com

"Swee Yong is a notable author on books covering real estate in Singapore. In this book, he provides a comprehensive yet succinct analysis on the trends in public and private housing in Singapore.

Readers will gain much foresight and views on the property market that befuddles most of us. Not only does the book address current issues but also those issues that could surface in the next 10 to 20 years, given the coming of age of the millennials and the zoomers as well as aging Gen Xs and baby boomers. What is most interesting is the inclusion of how new technology will change and shape our homes. It also gives you a glimpse of how Singapore may look like in the future as urban planning is key to the transformation of Singapore into a Smart City.

The book is a recommended read and I applaud Swee Yong for updating all of us who have a keen interest in Singapore property."

—Lee Chiwi
Chief Executive, PreceptsGroup

"Readers and followers of Ku Swee Yong will find his hallmark contrarian views; specifically probing questions and discomforting answers. As the virus rages and statistics about deaths, illnesses and displaced families multiply in this unprecedented crisis, he asks if we should become introspective instead.

Swee Yong posits that 'This tumultuous pandemic year has offered many of us a great opportunity for personal growth,' so he suggests that we study demographic shifts, technological disruptions and geo-political transformations that steamroll ahead despite this microscopic malaise assaulting global economies. Readers of this book will enjoy the nuggets of real estate gold in this engaging collection of thoughts, probes and evocations."

—Winston Lim
Architect and Managing Director, Winstudio Architects

THE FUTURE OF REAL ESTATE

THE FUTURE OF REAL ESTATE

KU SWEE YONG

Author of the bestselling *Real Estate Riches*

Marshall Cavendish
Business

© 2021 Ku Swee Yong

Reprinted 2021

Published by Marshall Cavendish Business
An imprint of Marshall Cavendish International

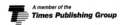

A member of the
Times Publishing Group

Other Marshall Cavendish Offices:
Marshall Cavendish Corporation, 800 Westchester Ave, Suite N-641, Rye Brook, NY 10573, USA • Marshall Cavendish International (Thailand) Co Ltd, 253 Asoke, 16th Floor, Sukhumvit 21 Road, Klongtoey Nua, Wattana, Bangkok 10110, Thailand • Marshall Cavendish (Malaysia) Sdn Bhd, Times Subang, Lot 46, Subang Hi-Tech Industrial Park, Batu Tiga, 40000 Shah Alam, Selangor Darul Ehsan, Malaysia

Marshall Cavendish is a registered trademark of Times Publishing Limited

National Library Board, Singapore Cataloguing-in-Publication Data

Name(s): Ku, Swee Yong.
Title: The future of real estate : what's next after new tech and Covid-19? / Ku Swee Yong.
Description: Singapore : Marshall Cavendish Business, [2021]
Identifier(s): OCN 1232210195 | ISBN 978-981-4928-44-1 (paperback)
Subject(s): LCSH: Real estate investment--Singapore. | Real property--Singapore. | Residential real estate--Singapore. | Commercial real estate--Singapore.
Classification: DDC 332.6324095957--dc23

Printed in Singapore

Dedicating my sixth book on real estate to you who asked:
"What does Swee Yong know about real estate?"

CONTENTS

Part 4: Commercial (Office & Retail) and Industrial

Part 5: Others - Investing Overseas, Debunking Myths & Wealth Transfer

About the Author

PREFACE

It has been three and a half years since the publication of my fifth book, *Preparing for a Property Upturn*. A relatively long break considering that the first book, *Real Estate Riches*, was published in early 2011 and by late 2017 the fifth book was already on the shelves. Six years to roll out the first five books and more than three years for this one.

I was happy with the success of *Preparing for a Property Upturn*, particularly Chapters 1 and 2 which highlighted the long-term issues of retirement for our ageing population coupled with the decaying values of old HDB flats with short remaining leases. Many readers and their families have benefitted from having deeper and wider discussions about their lifelong savings stuck in home ownership vis-à-vis their retirement adequacy. As more readers and families are concerned about this topic, I have included a few more chapters on public housing, including a policy proposal crafted with Prof Tay Kheng Soon and ex-Chief Economist of GIC Mr Yeoh Lam Keong, in this book.

Chapter 3 of *Preparing for a Property Upturn* presented challenges and proposals for the future of real estate. As Singapore's planners will be reviewing the country's Concept

Plan in 2021, I highlighted the need to look at our land use plans by considering the combined impact of new technologies that will disrupt our urban landscape in the next 20 to 30 years. The effects of two or three technological leaps will not be sufficient to force significant changes in the urban landscape. A dozen technological advancements in combination, say in the areas of 3D printing, autonomous vehicles, 5G communications, drones, education, e-commerce, blockchain, etc., will exert a strong demand on cities to adapt buildings and the urban landscape. Even the Chinese government's recent policy announcements for China's "14th Five-Year Plan for National Economic and Social Development and the Long-term Goals for 2035"[1] repeatedly stressed the importance of "in-depth integration" of technologies and industries, encouraging mergers and reorganisations for the sharing economy. Policy planners have started to recognise that policies need to take into account the combined impact of technological and societal changes rather than amend policies piecemeal based on each particular trend.

In the next two decades, the cities that are able to morph themselves to enjoy the benefits offered by the entire suite of new technologies will be the ones that thrive. The rest will fall into redundancy. Urban regeneration will be my key research focus area in the next few years. I will also embark on investment projects for the revitalisation of historically significant old towns in Japan, and possibly Europe.

In the past three years, I busied myself with real estate related work, attending to clients in Singapore and overseas markets through brokering transactions and providing research, consulting and advisory services. Some readers may know that I regularly post my observations during site visits as well as provide commentaries about the economy and real estate market on YouTube

---

1 "14th Five-Year Plan for National Economic and Social Development and the Long-term Goals for 2035", The State Council The People's Republic Of China, 3 November 2020, http://www.gov.cn/zhengce/2020-11/03/content_5556991.htm

http://bit.ly/KSYYouTube and Telegram http://bit.ly/KSYTele. Click subscribe and follow these channels for updates about the market.

Being an active real estate broker and analyst allows me to publish and create teaching materials for investors, full-time students and fellow real estate practitioners.

With the Singapore Management University, I was honoured to be able to jointly develop and teach the subject of real estate investments and finance with Emeritus Professor Francis Koh, a renowned professor of finance. With his support and four semesters of appreciative students, I was awarded the Lee Kong Chian School of Business Dean's Teaching Honour List Top Adjunct Faculty for two consecutive academic years.

In Ngee Ann Polytechnic, I developed and taught the module of real estate market research and statistics for three years. I also assisted the faculty members with developing educational materials for full-time students and adult learners. Two of the courses are on the mobile learning platform Gnowbe, which allows property agents to fulfil their Continuing Professional Development requirements through their phones and other mobile devices anywhere, anytime.

More recently, after the Circuit Breaker, I developed two new courses. One for adult learners who prefer to take online courses at their own pace named "Singapore Real Estate Fairy Tales – What's New After Covid-19?" on the Heuta Learners e-learning platform. (Readers who are interested in the Heuta Learners course may look at https://www.heutalearners.com/singaporerealestatekusweeyong)

Another course was created jointly with renowned Trust Specialist Mr Lee Chiwi of PreceptsGroup International. Titled "Wealth Transfer with Real Estate", we created this course in response to the demand from bankers and financial advisors who are assisting the growing numbers of retiree families drawing up their inheritance plans.

Starting in 2021, I will be reaching out to Community Centres around Singapore to conduct short talks on "Wealth Transfer & Your HDB Flat" and "Outlook for Singapore Real Estate after Covid-19". I hope to make information about real estate investments and wealth transfer widely available at an affordable cost to the general public.

Creating and delivering lessons in real estate and finance has contributed to my growth, as it has allowed me to learn a lot from my students. Everyone around me are my teachers, including the people I observe during my site visits, or when I am chilling out at Holland Village, or when looking at the retirees and families seated across Tanglin Halt Food Centre.

This tumultuous pandemic year has offered many of us a great opportunity for personal growth. For those of us not stuck in menial jobs, and those of us whose eyes are open, wide awake and with full awareness, this era of great learning will grow each of our souls tremendously, compensating for the stagnation the past 50 years of economic success has brought.

For those who are just stepping out of school, and attending virtual graduation ceremonies, the world wants you to continue learning. Despite half the world going into slow-motion in mid-2020, an abundance of lessons unfolded right in front of our eyes and lessons will continue to reveal themselves well beyond 2021. This will be a period of great learning and realisation. We need to assimilate our knowledge gained in school, with what is happening around the world now. Fresh graduates should continually reflect on the differences and similarities between the learning in schools and that beyond, and choose your next steps wisely.

For those who have been dealt an unkind blow by this pandemic, struggling with losses or looking for directions, I encourage you to continue growing your soul even as you mend your losses. The devil in this world will not go away until leaders learn to love the citizens and citizens learn to love the world. We have a long way to go before this world is healed.

This book would not be complete if I do not express my appreciation for everyone who has supported me with my work, my research, my teachings and my learnings: Catherine Thoo Sin Ling, Emeritus Professor Francis Koh Cher Chiew, Lai Yeu Huan, Alvin Mah, Tan Kok Keong, Elaina Olivia Chong, Chan Mun Wei, David Liew Yean Sin, Kannan Chandran, Yeoh Lam Keong, Professor Tay Kheng Soon, Makoto "Micky" Kojima, Valerie Toh Jao Jin, Vina Ip, Justin Chong Hou Shin, Hazel Tan En Lin, Pamela How Rui Ying, Joshua Toh Yi Xing, Joel Kam Jia Chuin, Swastik Agarwal, Soh Yun Yee, Law Yin Kai, Tan Guan Wei, Brandan Koh Yee Swee, Krystle Ng Ren Ying, Jolene Ng Hui Yi, Xavier Ling Shang Zhi, Yeoh Theng, Aloysius Ng Shi Hao, Dara Hanson, Benjamin Tan Ting Cher, Rachel Chan Min, Esther Ng Li Ting, Justin Wong Yi Jie, Sophia Chow Hui Ru, Wang Sijie, Yoon Zhen Yu and Tan Kit Yee.

In addition to the students who assisted me with research, analyses and writing, I would also like to thank editors Melvin Neo and Yeo Suan Futt for going through these pages and helping me to stay focused. Any errors or oversights in this book are probably mine. Since the passing of the anti-fake news law, better known in its short form as POFMA, I have decided to stay away from media interviews. Readers who wish to follow my market updates are welcome to contact me through social media and stay in touch on YouTube http://bit.ly/KSYYouTube and Telegram http://bit.ly/KSYTele.

Ku Swee Yong
January 2021

PART 1

NEW TECH, URBAN PLANNING, SMART CITY

1. Future of Singapore's Real Estate

Perhaps my views are expressed a tad too early. My analyses, forecasts and market calls are perhaps one to ten years ahead of their time, especially on the issues of ageing demographics and public housing.

Why am I doing this? I am simply trying to save investors from getting themselves into unprofitable investments. I hope to help investors avoid regrets.

In my second book *Building Your Real Estate Riches* published at the end of 2012, I discussed the risks and potential downsides of investing in small-sized strata non-residential properties such as small shops, small industrial units, small medical suites and small offices. From my third book *Real Estate Realities* published in mid-2014 to my fourth and fifth books, I warned about the hype of the High Speed Rail to Jurong, the Rapid Transit System to Woodlands and the excessive supply of properties in Malaysia, especially those in the Iskandar region.

For both the above forecasts and subsequent reminder-warnings that I wrote about, I received criticisms from unhappy property agents and even threats of legal action from developers.

But the facts speak for themselves. Even without Covid-19, many landlords of small retail shops, medical suites, industrial units and offices were suffering from long periods of vacancies and weak rentals. The Malaysian political flip-flops killed their housing market and those who have bought into the fluff of Jurong and Iskandar are mainly middle-income Singaporeans with lofty dreams and building castles in the air.

Most of the people who dislike my research label me as "negative" or "pessimistic". Occasionally, I get comments from trolls and people who deflect the discussions off at a tangent. For example, on the difficult discussions around retirement adequacy of retirees living in old HDB flats with deteriorating values, the trolls will alter the discussion by calling me divisive, accusing me of causing a rift in society. But these trolls have no ability nor interest to contribute to the discussions around the retirement adequacy of our ageing population staring at declining values of their old flats.

I am not doing this for extra clicks and likes. I am doing this to save investors and their families from financial pains. And that is the biggest motivation for me to keep writing and producing content, such as those on my Telegram channel (http://bit.ly/KSYTele) and Youtube channel (http://bit.ly/KSYYouTube).

So here I go again. In this lead chapter of my sixth book *The Future of Real Estate*, I will set out my forecasts for Singapore's property scene over the next 10 years by explaining the four key forces impacting, and imposing changes on, real estate.

1. Demographics and our ageing population

Within the next 10 years, we will see Generation Y (also known as the millennials) and Generation Z (i.e. the zoomers) dictate the rules about consumption and spending habits. According to broad definitions, in the year 2021, the millennials will be around 25 years to 40 years of age and the zoomers between 10 to 24 years of age.

By the year 2030, the millennials (around 34 to 49 years age) will be at their peak income, the zoomers will be mostly in the labour force, while Generation X (the generation after the post-World War 2 baby boomers and born between 1965 to 1980 who will be about 50 to 64 years old) will be stepping into retirement and beginning to draw on their CPF reserves.

Also in the year 2030, the baby boomers will be about 65 to 85 years old and will already be drawing down on their CPF Retirement Accounts. The generation before the baby boomers, also known as the "Silent Generation" that lived through the Great Depression and World War 2, will be passing on in larger and larger numbers. According to statistical models produced with several students from the Singapore Management University, we believe that by the year 2030, Singapore will see as many resident-deaths as we have resident-births (of about 30,000 each year). Beyond 2030, the number of deaths each year will exceed the number of live births. (Note: "Singapore resident" refers to both Singapore Citizens and Singapore Permanent Residents. The bulk of population data publicly available from Singstat refers to Singapore residents.)

Fig. 1 shows the cohorts of population, segmented by generations. We can see that all the cohorts from "25-29 years" to "60-64 years" number above 250,000 per cohort. This means that each year for 40 years from 2020 till 2060, more than 50,000 Singapore residents will celebrate their 65th birthday. In some years the number of additional 65-year-olds will increase by more than 60,000.

Fig. 1: Five-year age cohorts of Singapore Residents segmented by generation groupings.

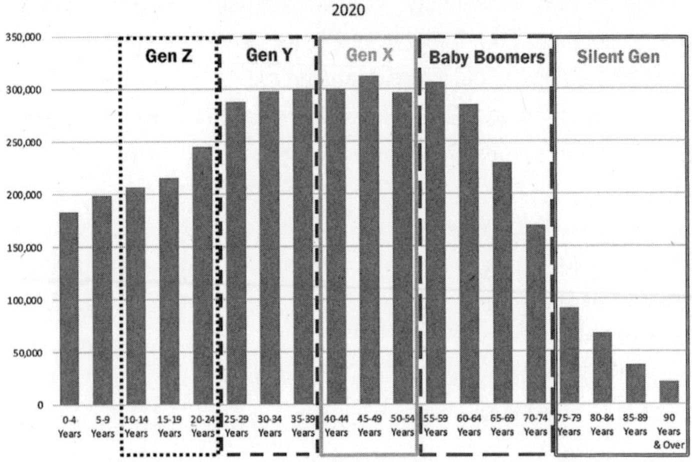

2020

Source: Singstat, International Property Advisor

Why are these numbers important?

Apart from the often-touted concern about the rapidly declining "old age support ratio", we have a seldom-mentioned issue of real estate wealth transfer.

The Gen Y and Gen Z will face a heavier and heavier burden as the old age support ratio declines. This is defined as the number of residents between the age of 20 to 64 (considered economically active) who will support each resident above age 65 (considered economically inactive). In the year 2020, there are 3.7 residents between age 20 to 64 supporting each resident above age 65. When we arrive at 2030, there will only be 2.4 residents of age 20 to 64 supporting each resident aged 65 and above.

The sharp drop from 3.7 to 2.4 is due to a combination of a large increase in the number of residents aged 65 and above and a decrease in the number of residents aged 20 to 64. This has serious consequences for the drawdown of CPF funds versus the contributions to CPF funds. In addition, I am concerned about whether we have sufficient capacity for healthcare services and facilities to meet the big increase in demand from retirees. We need to ramp up building more healthcare infrastructure and improving our capabilities and services immediately or we will be caught off-guard with a lack of capacity and sky-rocketing healthcare costs. Keep in mind that many of our doctors, nurses and healthcare workers are also in the ageing baby boomer and Gen X groups and will leave the workforce.

I digress. The CPF and healthcare issues are critical but they fall outside the realm of real estate.

The biggest issue that is caused by the rapidly ageing society and which affects a vast majority of families is this: real estate wealth transfer. For the last five decades, our grandparents and parents have been using their homes as the main store of retirement wealth. With the swelling numbers of retirees ageing towards their demise (median age of death being about 86 for those who are alive at age 65), I am expecting to see a lot more inherited properties that are put up for resale.

Resident-deaths have increased from 17,600 in the year 2010 to about 21,400 in 2019. As explained earlier in this chapter, by the year 2030 the annual number of resident deaths is forecast to exceed 30,000. Within the next 10 years, we should expect to see a total of about 250,000 deaths. What will happen to the "store of wealth" belonging to those who pass away?

On average, 90% of us are home owners and 80% of residents own and live in HDB flats. The passing away of the second parent would, in high probability, result in a HDB flat that would be transferred to the surviving children. And in all likelihood, the surviving children are also owners of private properties or HDB flats. Based on current laws, no one is allowed to have their name registered in more than one HDB flat. This and other considerations mean that most families end up selling the flats bequeathed by their parents, so that the beneficiaries can share the cash proceeds from the sale of the flats. And by that time, how many will be in the market to buy these, probably 20 to 30-year-old flats?

First time home buyers in the year 2030 will be largely made up of zoomers with a few late buyers from the millennials group. With reference to Fig. 1, it is clear that the total number of zoomers who are eligible and can afford to buy homes might count for fewer than the 30,000 deaths of baby boomers and Silent Gens.

Furthermore, the millennials, followed by zoomers, are less inclined than the generations before them to marry before 30, to have children or rush to own a property. My grandparents and parents would save as much as they can and forgo luxuries in order to own a flat as soon as they can afford. The millennials and zoomers will probably prioritise holidays and enriching their life experience before saving up on the downpayment required for their homes. These generations will have different lifestyles, hoard less material goods and prefer living purposeful lives rather than chasing papers or financial wealth. They also view renting and home-sharing more favourably than being handcuffed to a long-term home loan.

There is also the question of affordability. Given that the iron-rice-bowl jobs of yore have been replaced by an increasing proportion of short-term contract work, the millennials today and zoomers in 2030 may not be able to afford a property until they have worked longer to save up for their first home.

Conceivably home prices could drop significantly, due to the degradation of lease, allowing more zoomers to enter the residential market early. In addition, inheritance handed down from Silent Gen and baby boomers could be passed on to zoomers to help them with downpayments for their first homes.

No matter how we slice the numbers, two outcomes are certain from the ageing demographics trend.

The passing of Silent Gen and baby boomers will release thousands of resale flats and private residences to the market every year, and we do not have sufficient demand due to the lower demand from the relatively small number of zoomers. We could of course open our doors wide and welcome more foreigners to take on citizenship here. But foreigners will come in droves only if we can create jobs. At this point, the outlook of the post-Covid-19 economy and our ability to generate a lot more jobs than before 2019 to attract quality foreign talent, is at best murky.

The second outcome of the ageing demographics is a shortage of affordable good quality senior housing. On this front, the government's efforts seem tentative at best. In 2014, Kampung Admiralty was launched by HDB as Singapore's first "integrated retirement community" project.[1] It also won several international accolades. However, there were only 100 flats in the development. HDB recently launched the first "assisted living HDB flats" for seniors over 65 years old which included basic healthcare services.[2] But as a trial, it is limited to 160 flats. For the past decade, HDB has also launched more studio apartments, 2-room flats and 2-room Flexi flats catering to seniors who wish to "right size" their abodes. At just below 3,000 units a year, it could have been sufficient for the last few years but compared to the more than 50,000 residents who

---

1 "Kampung Admiralty", Wikipedia, https://en.wikipedia.org/wiki/Kampung_Admiralty
2 Michelle Ng, "Singapore's first assisted living HDB flats for seniors to launch in Bukit Batok in Feb 2021 BTO exercise", *The Straits Times*, 10 December 2020, https://www.straitstimes.com/singapore/housing/singapores-first-assisted-living-hdb-flats-for-seniors-to-launch-in-bukit-batok-in

will celebrate their 65th birthday each year from 2020, it might not be enough.

Policy makers could have one concern. If the supply of old-age housing were abundant and affordable, it could lead many retirees to downsize and encash their old 4-room and 5-room flats. This could add even more downward pressure to the diminishing resale value of old HDB flats and affect the valuations of all public housing islandwide. This could be a consequence the planners want to avoid.

Further details will be discussed in Chapter 6 on public housing, where Singapore's ageing demographics and its impact on the public housing resale market are further elaborated and explained.

2. Politics and external market environment

When we gaze into the crystal ball about Singapore's real estate, we need to pay close attention to the economy, to jobs growth, to demographic trends and to what policy makers around the world are doing. Singapore being a very open economy with a tiny domestic market will be susceptible to major actions taken by the global heavyweights. For example, when the USA decided to pull out of the Trans-Pacific Partnership, it was negative for Singapore's status as a trade hub. And when the USA tightened up on Chinese companies operating in the USA, Singapore could conceivably benefit if Chinese companies expanded their operations here.

However, it would be far-fetched to link every action taken by the economic superpowers back to their impact on the Singapore real estate market. Most of these ripples will just flow by although a fraction may gather strength and turn into waves, affecting us in the immediate term, some over the long term. A fraction of them will impact the Singapore economy, such as our attractiveness for capital and for global talent. And a smaller subset will eventually impact real estate. What is important is to be cognizant, to be aware, of what is happening around us outside of Singapore.

A recent major development for Asia came in the form of the RCEP, or Regional Comprehensive Economic Partnership. This agreement signed between Australia, Brunei, Cambodia, China, Indonesia, Japan, Laos, Malaysia, Myanmar, New Zealand, the Philippines, Singapore, South Korea, Thailand, and Vietnam is the first trade agreement between the three North Asian economic powers (China, Japan and South Korea). These 15 countries account for 30% of the world's population (2.2 billion people) and 30% of global GDP (US$26 trillion).[3]

Being a very open economy and a long-time proponent of free trade, Singapore may not derive a lot of direct benefits from the RCEP. On the other hand, if this deal increases trade between the other 14 nations north and south of us, trades and goods will still flow through the Singapore hub. Then again, not everything is hunky dory as we have recently witnessed the trade spats between Australia and China, two members of the RCEP.

Developments within China will get even more interesting in the next decade. The institutional real estate world has been waiting for Beijing to approve the listings of China Real Estate Investment Trusts or C-REITs. The market value of C-REITs is estimated to be over US$1 trillion. C-REITs will initially be limited to infrastructure real estate such as toll roads, data centres and utilities assets.

Announced in November 2020, China's 14th Five-Year Plan for National Economic and Social Development and the Long-term Goals for 2035 is what I would describe as bold. The policy planners are proposing "in-depth integration" of industries such as artificial

---

3 "Regional Comprehensive Economic Partnership", *Wikipedia*, https://en.wikipedia.org/wiki/Regional_Comprehensive_Economic_Partnership

intelligence, internet, big data, advanced manufacturing, etc. What struck me was the recognition that the future sharing-economy and platform-economy requires a multi-disciplinary approach and Beijing is strongly promoting this point across all industries and services sectors.

The demand for new generation infrastructure and services will drive jobs, which will stimulate consumer demand. New infrastructure such as next-generation data networks, 5G telecommunications and applications, charging and battery swap stations for vehicles, clean energy, etc. combine real estate with science and technology. Such investments will help China to further modernise and upgrade the country's capabilities. The introduction of C-REITs will be a major source of financing for the new infrastructure roll out.

While China plans her growth in the new world, many other countries are wary of China's capabilities, financial prowess and international influence. The new President of the United States, Mr Joseph Biden Jr, is one who is wary about China's ascension on the world stage. Biden is way more diplomatic than Trump and is expected to improve US foreign relations that were soured under Trump's leadership (or lack of). But we should expect trade spats between China and the USA to continue as long as Biden feels the threat of China expanding its influence and control over on the Asian side of the Pacific Ocean.

The rise of China's influence is both a positive (e.g. a very wealthy and growing consumer market) and a worry for her neighbours: South Korea, Japan, Taiwan and Hong Kong. Political leaders are keen to do business with China but are concerned about their exporters' strong reliance on the Chinese market. Australian wine and agriculture exporters paid the price recently when import duties were slapped on their products.

Over in Japan, the longest serving Prime Minister, Mr Shinzo Abe, resigned in August 2020 after implementing major economic reforms known as "Abenomics". His successor, Mr Yoshihide Suga, is likely to continue with opening up the Japanese market to the world but having taken over in the midst of the Covid-19 pandemic and with trillions of Japanese Yen spent on the Olympics, will he be able to steer the country to continue growing? Thus far, he has responded swiftly to the economic pains by calling for a third supplementary Covid-19 budget of over JPY10-15 trillion (S$128-193 billion) for Green and Environment funding, digital transformation and the promotion of urban to rural migration. Reversing migration flows by allowing more people to work remotely in rural areas, outside commercial hubs will bring major benefits in decongesting big cities and improving lifestyles. As I am involved in a project to revitalise a 1,400-year-old town, this is a positive step which I will be watching closely. Investors who are keen to join me on this journey can contact me for a discussion.

International trade spats will not be limited to China and the USA. Or China and Australia. Post-Covid-19, many countries have become more nationalistic and inward-looking, seeking to protect their domestic markets over cheaper imports. We have also witnessed a very long-drawn impasse between the United Kingdom and Europe over the terms of international trade after the UK leaves the European Union. The fallout of Brexit, its repercussions on labour, goods and services moving between the UK and Europe, demand in the UK real estate market, etc. will play out over the next two years.

Nearer home in ASEAN, there are many pockets of flux. The political situation in Thailand is worrisome. Malaysia's politics is likened to flipping roti pratas and the spread of the coronavirus seems unstoppable even as we cross into 2021. The pandemic is also causing a slowdown in the major consumer markets of Indonesia and the Philippines. It seems that Cambodia and Vietnam are the two economies still running almost like normal, just short of international tourism and transport markets.

The eventual outcomes of these macro, global changes are not easy to predict. As investors, we should be cognizant that these changes are happening and be aware that they might impact us in Singapore.

After the General Election 2020, the Minister for National Development (MND) was changed to Mr Desmond Lee. This is the fourth National Development minister in the last 10 years as the minister was also changed after General Election 2011, and 2015. While I expect that the new minister will maintain consistency with policies, I am watching out for major shifts in developments of public housing, new towns and infrastructure.

I appreciate the ex-National Development Minister Lawrence Wong's decisions and actions to maintain stability in the property market, for example in jointly curbing speculation with the Finance Minister by introducing additional cooling measures in July 2018. I also credit him with reminding Singaporeans that HDB flats will depreciate to zero value at the end of 99 years of lease. After five decades of building this country, it was appropriate to set the expectations of overly-government-reliant Singaporeans that the government will bail them out of depreciating HDB values. Singaporeans have probably forgotten that the contracts they signed with the HDB include an Agreement for Lease and a Memorandum of Lease. Somehow, there is an expectation that our flats' values are sufficiently high to act as a nest-egg for two to three decades of retirement, that there will also be substantial wealth in the HDB "asset" to hand down to our descendants.

I cannot guess the rationale for changing the national development minister in the middle of a pandemic, especially when the construction industry is reeling from the challenges of foreign workers and their dormitories, construction-related accidents and deaths, delays to public housing projects, etc. I am more concerned that each change of minister may shift some goals and introduce new mega-projects. Since the Jurong Lake District (JLD) was announced as a mega-development area in 2008, there have been half a dozen more projects announced with fanfare and rosy promises of a prosperous future. The Buona Vista One-North precinct has been under development for the past 20 years and we have merely developed about 50% of the sites available. The JLD is less than half developed and we see the promises of the High Speed Rail has been derailed. So, what might the future look like for JLD, given that budgets and focus are also spread across to the nearby Jurong Innovation District, Tengah Forest Town and Greater Southern Waterfront? Will the new minister put more energy and budget on all these projects that were kicked off by previous ministers, or will he champion yet another new precinct such as Simpang, Marina East or Paya Lebar Airbase? Will he focus attention on the existing towns such as Ang Mo Kio and Bukit Panjang or the redevelopment of Tanglin Halt?

Mr Desmond Lee's early actions since taking over the national development portfolio has been to change the Chief Executive Officers of the HDB and the Building and Construction Authority. He has also shared his concerns about how HDB flats in prime locations may be priced affordably but yet avoid having tax payers sponsor million-dollar windfalls, i.e. the "lottery effect", for a few lucky citizens. However, as at the end of 2020, the minister has not given any indications about how he views the value depreciation of old HDB flats. Within 10 years, there will be more than 500,000 HDB flats that are more than 40 years old. So while the number of retiree households grow quickly, their retirement nest eggs are quickly shrinking. In my opinion, the HDB value decay is a most pressing issue which has to be dealt with without delay.

Under this minister's watch, the Concept Plan 2021 will be released. It is a strategic land use plan which shapes Singapore's development for the next 40 to 50 years. Within the time horizon for this plan, over a hundred thousand HDB flats will reach the end of their 99-year lease.

Let us keep tabs on the new minister's vision in the Concept Plan 2021 as we keep an eye on the global macro-economic shifts that may affect Singapore.

Note: A box story is included at the end of this chapter which briefly outlines a concept plan proposal for the redevelopment of Paya Lebar Airport. This proposal was jointly created by David Liew Sin Yean, Chan Mun Wei, Elaina Olivia Chong and myself. It is a vision of what we think Singapore's urban development direction should head towards:

a. The urban environment should support the human activities of live, work, play, learn, farm and heal.
b. Singapore is already almost 100% urbanised, we should re-grow and expand green areas to absorb carbon and reduce our country's carbon footprint.

3. The combined impact of technological disruptions on real estate

As discussed in Chapter 3 of my fifth book *Preparing for a Property Upturn,* "Concept Plan 2021: What's Next for Singapore's Built Environment?", there are several trends in technology which deserve watching closely. On their own, the new technologies will impact real estate to a negligible extent. However, in order for major cities to remain competitive, they will need to upgrade to incorporate the list of new technologies being introduced today. Adopting all the technology changes within, say, a span of 10 years will force city planners and policy makers to make a lot of adjustments to the urban landscape. In the next two to three decades, major cities around the world could look like giant construction sites in various stages of "renovation", retrofits or even extensive regeneration (i.e. demolitions and construction).

The technology changes include the following:

a. Autonomous vehicles (cars, buses and trucks). To move around by themselves, autonomous (or driverless) vehicles require sensors built into streets, traffic junctions, buildings, bus-stops and other infrastructure within a city. The increase in adoption of autonomous vehicles will make carparks somewhat irrelevant and will increase the need for pick-up and drop-off points in buildings. Some in-building carparks may be renovated to serve that purpose, but most of the carpark lots (especially those in condominiums) will become dead space. In most countries, excess carpark lots may be repurposed for other uses. But in Singapore, land use regulations and guidelines for Gross Floor Area and Plot Ratio will have to be changed before carparks can be converted into other uses. As passengers can call on these vehicles through mobile apps, the adoption of autonomous vehicles is expected to reduce car ownership mainly to the large transportation companies. In addition, road safety will be enhanced as the incidences of reckless driving and driving under the influence of drugs and alcohol will drop significantly.

b. Electric vehicles and battery swap stations. The current method of tethering an electric car to a power point and charging its batteries for a few hours may soon be made redundant by "battery swap stations" where an autonomous vehicle could align itself within the station where robotic arms then replace the spent batteries with fresh ones. Electric vehicles have up to 80% fewer moving parts. Coupled with autonomous vehicles which will reduce car ownership to that being owned by a few large transportation and logistics companies, we could expect a big reduction in automotive maintenance and repair shops, and fewer jobs for mechanics. In future, large scale industrial buildings for automotive repairs, such as Ang Mo Kio Autopoint and Sin Ming AutoCity, will have to shrink. And perhaps petrol kiosks might be renovated to provide battery swapping services.

c. Drones for transporting goods and humans are being trialled in many parts of the world. Here in Singapore, German urban air-mobility company Volocopter announced that they will start an air-taxi service by the year 2023. How many take-off/landing stations will be built? Would it be autonomous or would it include a human pilot? How many beacons would have to be installed for navigation? How many buildings or open spaces would have to be reconfigured with take-off/landing facilities? What safety features and accident prevention measures might have to be installed?

d. Remote teaching and online learning have been growing ever so slowly in the last 50 years. The British Broadcasting Corporation started to air the UK Open University courses through television and radio in 1971. But the demand for in-class learning never diminished because learning in class provides learners with richer experience and higher quality learning. However, the advent of high-speed internet and rich multimedia content has pushed more and more learning content online and in the past 10 years, MOOC, or Massive Open Online Courses, has taken off in a big way. Children and adult learners alike are taking lessons and getting tutored online, especially after Covid-19 and global lockdowns pushed our lives onto the internet cloud. The introduction of 5G wireless technology will allow schools to bring even richer content to learners. All the technological advancements will lead to one thing: the need for lecture halls in schools and universities will diminish. Especially in Singapore where land is expensive, private schools in the CBD and fringe of CBD could expand their student enrolment and still reduce the commercial space they occupy if they put more education content online. Since Covid-19, many foreign students are taking classes from their home cities without stepping into Singapore. Expect more commercial space to be given up as private education providers shift to online learning.

e. The above are merely four examples out of a list of a dozen technology-led disruptions to real estate. Others include PropTech (which also covers property maintenance and construction), 3D printing for manufacturing, alternative energy, security technology, artificial intelligence, robotics, and bio-sensors that allow humans to interact with the built-environment and robots. The application of blockchain technology to real estate will break lumpy real estate deals into smaller fractions or tokens. Every single real estate asset can be financially and legally re-structured into fractional ownership, such as a mini-REIT owned by many people. This will open up real estate investments to a wider pool of mass market investors and transform real estate from being illiquid and lumpy to a low-cost investment product that investors can trade daily. In this field, the Japanese and Koreans are leading the pack. A recent example is Kasa Korea's investment into an office building in Gangnam, Seoul where individual investors on the Kasa mobile app can invest from KRW5,000 (about S$6.10) per unit of investment. Investors can subsequently trade the investment units on the mobile app or hold the units so as to receive rental income every three months.

The combined impact of these technologies on real estate will be big, and will be global. They will force real estate to change.

With most developed nations pushing into digital transformation, the pace of technology adoption will speed up even more. Covid-19 has made technology adoption more urgent. And 5G wireless networks will enable digital interactions to be smoother, faster and richer. The combination of technological disruptions compel city planners and policy makers to adapt their urban plans even more quickly. Changes to the built environment (i.e. buildings, streetscape, urban layout) will happen on a massive scale within the next 10 years.

Cities unable or slow to recognize and make necessary alterations will lose competitiveness in the global race for investments, jobs and growth.

Cities and countries which are able to adapt to the changes forced by tech-disruptions will regenerate themselves with improved infrastructure, buildings, urban landscapes and neighbourhoods. The improved efficiency will provide businesses and trades with a superior edge. Livability will be enhanced and the cities will be magnets for global top talents and their families. The longevity and relevance of these cities will be boosted.

However, at the same time, adopting such technology changes will render some types of real estate assets useless or irrelevant. For example, we are already seeing the obvious impact of ecommerce on the increasing number of vacant retail shops. Car-sharing and online education are starting to empty out car parks and lecture halls. As people around the world "migrate" their lives more and more onto the internet, less real estate will be required on the ground and more space will be required in the cloud. On one hand, physical floor space will be made redundant while on the other, data centres will grow in prominence.

I will be researching this topic extensively over the next few years. The overarching questions are: *Are major cities prepared for the changes forced upon them by a combination of technological disruptions? How do we reconfigure existing cities to adapt to new technologies?* Understanding how a handful of technological improvements will force changes on existing buildings and the urban environment will allow city planners to start tweaking designs of entire cities, as well as transforming and renovating buildings to be fit for future tech-savvy users.

With technology, nothing will be the same as before. We need to reconfigure and regenerate cities. There is no turning back. Especially not after Covid-19.

4. A post-Covid-19 world of real estate

According to Dictionary.com, the People's Choice 2020 Word of the Year is "unprecedented".

I agree. And I reminded my audience and readers of my social media posts about its meaning:

> "Without previous instance; never before known or experienced; unexampled or unparalleled"

Since we describe the Covid-19 pandemic and the economic turbulence it has caused us as "unprecedented", I cannot understand why economists, policy makers and financiers kept on drawing parallels between this crisis and previous economic downturns such as the Lehman Crisis (in 2008), SARS (in 2003), Asian Financial Crisis (in 1997) and even The Great Depression (in 1929). If an event has never happened before, drawing on past experience will only bring wrong conclusions. And that might have been why some governments became complacent and failed to tame the pandemic early.

Look at this pandemic with fresh eyes. Test all scenarios. Including the impossible, such as crude oil trading at *negative* US$30 a barrel.

As a chemist and not a person trained in traditional economics, I probably peer into the murky post-Covid-19 world with more objectivity than analysts who study boom-bust cycles. This final section of the chapter will wrap up with my murky vision about what may be in store for various real estate segments.

Covid-19 has brought a lot of pain and suffering to individuals and communities around the world. It has also brought out the best examples of love and compassion exchanged between people. The pandemic also revealed much kindness and kampung spirit in Singapore. But it has also laid bare our weaknesses: a trade hub caught with broken supply chains, squabbles over toilet rolls, segmenting a third class of people in Singapore – the migrant workers – by categorising them as being outside of our "local community" as if they existed outside our shores.

On the real estate front, after the initial slew of grants to protect jobs and businesses, the government sought to protect tenants by providing rental waivers, to protect landlords by allowing debt moratoriums and increasing the borrowing capacity of REITs (Real Estate Investment Trusts), and to protect home owners also by extending moratoriums on mortgages. These special laws were a relief for many businesses but the drop in business was not sufficient to prevent others from closing shop. New businesses, start-ups, retailers and tourism operators are some examples that have closed within the second half of 2020. With the special laws and jobs support schemes running out in early 2021, many businesses are on the cusp: to stay open with an optimistic view that the economic upturn will be swift, or to wind down because a slow improvement in the economy will still bleed the business dry. Whatever the case, as long as businesses are in flux, real estate will be impacted.

Hospitality segment

The categories of real estate most impacted by the pandemic are related to hospitality, travel and tourism. Real estate assets such as hotels, convention and exhibition centres, attractions, museums, casinos and theme parks have suffered. The worst-hit locations close to us are resort cities such as Phuket, Penang, Langkawi and Bali. Singapore is a small country with a big tourism services sector. But without a domestic tourism market, a lot of our assets were laid bare causing the government to pump in billions of dollars to keep about half the hotels operating with people arriving on "Stay Home Notice" or SHN arrangements. Changi and Seletar airports, the cruise centres and multiple bus stations linked to overland transport to Malaysia are other examples of assets with poor utilization.

Now that we have introduced incentives for staycations and for visiting attractions, activity has seeped back into the hotels (and also that campsite in Changi Airport). The local staycation numbers will not be sufficient to make up for the foreign visitors we had in 2019 (more than 19 million) but it supports jobs as well as provides relief for Singaporeans' travel sickness.

Even with the vaccine being rolled out across the world, I think Singapore's hotel and serviced apartment valuations will take a significant cut in 2021, especially once the government-supported SHN arrangements are withdrawn this year and before global travel recovers. Despite the high prices reflected in an ultra-optimistic stock market, I believe that real estate investors should hold back from investing in Singapore's hospitality assets and the travel sector in 2021. However, in countries with high population and where domestic tourism is strong, such as Japan, France and the UK, the vaccine will help hotel operators to recover much quicker.

Investors should also avoid companies and REITs with significant holdings of properties related to meetings and conventions. The days of the finance industry organising regular events such as Corporate Days and economic outlook seminars in convention centres and hotel ballrooms are over. Lockdowns during the pandemic have forced rapid upgrades in video conferencing technology, helping convert most business conferences to online meetings.

Another business sector dependent on foreign visitors is the entertainment sector. Restrictions on nightclubs and bars are slowly being lifted. But even if they were allowed to resume business as before in 2019, there will not be sufficient business to keep the sector healthy if visitor arrivals do not recover within a year. Some of the operators have converted their businesses to restaurants while famous nightclub Zouk has introduced a cycling gym and a cinema in its premises. For the rest who are unable to adapt their premises to other businesses or do not have sufficient manpower to do so, I believe that more than 50% of these nightclubs and bars (such as those in Orchard Towers, Cuppage Plaza, Orchard Plaza and Lucky Plaza) will close for good.

Retail segment

Most of these entertainment businesses occupy retail space. Demand for retail space was already anaemic even before Covid-19 hit us. However, given the long road to business, jobs and income recovery, demand for retail space is likely to shrink another 10%, i.e. a reduction of about six million sqft, especially as ecommerce adoption grows. The pandemic has not only forced consumers onto ecommerce platforms quickly, it has boosted the speed and improved the efficiency of the last-mile delivery to our homes and offices.

Food & Beverage services, which take up a significant 20-30% of all retail space, have backward-integrated into a catering-style business model, delivering their menu from cloud kitchens straight to our homes. Consumer goods manufacturers and retailers have realigned their product offerings, expanded their online presence and fulfilment capabilities to bring convenience to customers.

Such realignment of business operations will change the need for retail space. F&B outlets can grow their revenues by expanding their central kitchens in industrial buildings. Supermarkets do not need to hold too much stock in their stores, especially for heavy and bulky non-perishable items which take up space. For most of us, online shopping has become a habit and we will not revert back to the past even after the world is immune to the coronavirus. Put in another way, I have already "invested" time and energy to learn and enjoy the convenience of ecommerce, so it is highly unlikely that I will delete the FairPrice app on my phone and revert to purchasing detergents or mineral water or rice at the physical FairPrice supermarket.

This does not mean that retail is going to die. We should refrain from using extreme descriptions such as the phrase "retail apocalypse". Retail space for services such as healthcare, tailors and hairdressers will still be needed. Consumers will still enjoy going out, making a trip out to the neighbourhood market or visit Orchard Road to take a look-see. But what they spend on will be changed. They might not be shopping for goods given that they can easily compare products and prices online and getting them delivered to their doorsteps the next day.

So, retail will not die. But we would be blind if we could not recognise that retail space demand will shrink, significantly. Vacancies in what used to be very popular hangouts such as Centrepoint and Far East Plaza are still increasing, one year after Covid-19 arrived. There is simply too much retail space in Singapore. Especially when visitor arrivals will take a few years to recover to the 19.1 million in 2019. Landlords who own retail space may have to brace for a permanent reduction in rental income, with sporadic periods of zero rental income for their shops.

This global pandemic has caused our lifestyles to change and technology has made the pandemic a little more tolerable. But now that we have been forced to adapt and have gotten used to the changes, we can see that the changes can be sticky and can become a "normal" permanent feature of our lives quickly.

Office segment

It is not just for ecommerce and retail. Many jobs have also been transformed permanently. Some of those who lost their jobs in retail sales went on to find jobs in online delivery and fulfilment. Many workers from the travel industry have moved on to healthcare services, content creation, services, etc. Many workers have invested time, money and energy in reskilling themselves and they have moved on from their previous roles.

Billions of dollars have been spent by corporations, with significant support from governments, to upgrade their capabilities. Businesses, corporations and governments have invested heavily in infrastructure to allow the work-from-home, study-from-home and stay-at-home economy to operate smoothly.

With all these investments, workers and organisations alike want to see a payback on investments. Mr Bill Gates of Microsoft fame has predicted that 50% of business travel will permanently disappear, probably because Microsoft is boosting their investments in their online meeting and office collaboration tools such as Microsoft 365 and Teams.

According to various surveys and corporate announcements, the Work From Home (WFH) or Work Anywhere trend is set to be a permanent feature for many organisations. Many employers indicated that they will provide or reimburse remote-working expenses such as internet bills, laptops, mobile phones and even home fit-outs. They are reconfiguring their work processes and giving more flexibility for both onsite and remote working.

After the lockdowns in many countries, perhaps having had a positive experience with employee productivity, large companies such as Mizuho Bank, Dell, Google, Facebook, Standard Chartered, etc. have announced flexible working plans allowing a large percentage of their employees to work outside their designated office locations. A sampling of recent news headlines:

> *The Edge Singapore*, 16 December 2020, "8 in 10 Singapore employees prefer to work from home, but are employers equally keen?"[4]

> CNBC, 17 November 2020, "Bill Gates says more than 50% of business travel will disappear in post-coronavirus world"[5]

> *The Business Times,* 20November 2020, "Mizuho to cut Singapore office space on work-from-home success: sources"[6]

> Bloomberg, 5 November 2020, "StanChart Unveils Permanent Move to Flexible Working From 2021"[7]

By allowing a fraction of their employees to Work Anywhere, many large firms will move to shrink office footprint. On the ground, we are already hearing about CEOs and CFOs of large corporations pondering about increasing shareholder value by planning to cut costs on office rentals. In Singapore, even if only 10%, or 7.7 million sqft, of office space were given up by current occupiers, the overall vacancy of office space will increase from 12% to 20%. That will

---

4 Ng Qi Siang, "8 in 10 Singapore employees prefer to work from home, but are employers equally keen?", *The Edge Singapore*, 16 December 2020, https://www.theedgesingapore. com/news/future-economy/8-10-singapore-employees-prefer-work-home-are-employers-equally-keen

5 Noah Higgins-Dunn, "Bill Gates says more than 50% of business travel will disappear in post-coronavirus world", CNBC, 17 November 2020, https://www.cnbc.com/2020/11/17/ coronavirus-bill-gates-says-more-than-50percent-of-business-travel-will-disappear-long-term.html

6 "Mizuho to cut Singapore office space on work-from-home success: sources", *The Business Times*, 20 November 2020, https://www.businesstimes.com.sg/real-estate/mizuho-to-cut-singapore-office-space-on-work-from-home-success-sources

7 Harry Wilson, "StanChart Unveils Permanent Move to Flexible Working From 2021", Bloomberg, 5 November 2020, https://www.bloomberg.com/news/articles/2020-11-05/ stanchart-unveils-permanent-move-to-flexible-working-from-2021

be a record high vacancy surpassing all the previous economic recessions such as during SARS and the Lehman Crisis.

Furthermore, investors in the office segment should keep an eye on flexible office space solutions and the moves of co-working office operators. There are more than 10 million square feet of vacant offices looking for tenants now. Seeing an increase in vacant offices and the challenges in filling them with tenants, many large landlords such as Capitaland and City Developments have converted vacant office space in their buildings into co-working spaces. These spaces are classified as "occupied" even though they are still looking for tenants who are the real users of the spaces. Smaller landlords who have difficulties renting out their office space and industrial B1 space have done the same. And post-Circuit Breaker, we have also seen hotels and restaurants jumping into the co-working space business.

But is there sufficient new demand to fill the existing vacant offices and co-working spaces? Real estate consultants and landlords are probably keeping mum on this even as data from office REITs and current contract negotiations are starting to show that office space is being given up and consolidated. The outlook leans on the side of a permanent shift to have a fraction of office workers not returning to their premises. I believe this is a fracture in demand that will take many more years of economic growth to fill. And in the meantime, we also have to brace ourselves for several large commercial projects adding more office supply.

Take this thinking one step further for Singapore as a regional and global business hub. Our office sector could lose more tenants given the advanced telecommunications tools that allow high value employees to work anywhere. For example, in the insurance and banking businesses, jobs that can be done outside offices such as "underwriter, claims reviewer, administrator" could also be done from the same employees' homes in Malaysia, Australia, Philippines, India and China. Just as credit card call centres are mainly operated from outside Singapore, business communications platforms such as Zoom, WebEx, Teams, Meet and Lark are supporting corporations to allow their workers to Work Anywhere. Soon we might even see foreign employees displacing Singaporeans from their jobs without having to set foot here nor having to apply for Employment Passes in Singapore.

A question nags me: with Work Anywhere arrangements, the CBD is likely to be less congested. Add weaker office demand. Add the existing 11 million sqft of vacant offices and add more than 8 million sqft of office space under construction. Do we really need to expand regional financial and business hubs such as Jurong East, Woodlands and Paya Lebar to decongest the CBD and bring jobs closer to homes when many jobs could be DONE FROM HOME?

Residential segment

Which brings me to the point about the potential of residential rentals in Singapore. If the future of work includes a significant, say more than 10%, share of workers who are able to Work Anywhere, where would the demand for residential rentals come from?

The pandemic has created an overall reduction of 172,000 jobs in 2020. As such, for the 12 months ended June 2020, we witnessed the first overall population decline of 17,800 since SARS in 2003. The overall population decline was mainly due to a loss of 35,800 pass holders and offset by an increase of 18,000 Singapore Citizens and Permanent Residents. In these numbers above, how many are tenants of residential properties?

The number of jobs lost would have been worse if not for the tens of thousands of "ambassadors" for social distancing and healthcare services, traineeships and guardians for entry control at tens of thousands of entrances of buildings. Even with the massive government support for jobs, the citizen unemployment rate hit an 11-year high of 4.5% at the end of December 2020.

Going forward, as social controls are relaxed after more people are vaccinated, many of these jobs will not be needed. With the population vaccinated, will jobs in retail, tourism, airlines, hotels, conventions, performing arts, etc. recover quickly? Perhaps the long queues for bubble tea and toilet paper in 2020 may turn into queues for jobs in 2021.

When jobs do return, given the high local unemployment, Singaporeans will be prioritised over foreign talent. And since 90% of Singaporean households are home owners, will there be sufficient tenants to rent the vacant homes? In 2020, there are 1.48 million dwelling units (i.e. HDB flats and private residences) and 1.37 million households. Some households, such as three-generation families, live together and therefore 1.37 million households occupy fewer than 1.2 million dwelling units. There are around 300,000 dwelling units which are available for rent and many of these owners may be stretched to pay their mortgages if the apartments are vacant for extended periods. And we have not counted the stock of bedrooms, mostly in HDB flats, that are seeking tenants too.

So, where will the tenants come from? When will they return?

I will pay close attention to jobs creation. But investors should also be mindful that there are around 100,000 HDB flats and private residences which will be completed by 2024. Do also be cognizant that we are swimming against the tide of ageing demographics with an increasing number of downgraders and resale units due to inheritance.

Fig. 2: total population and residential units in Singapore from year 2000 to 2020

Year	Population ('000)			Annual Difference ('000)			Private Residential Units		EC Units		Public Residential Units		Total Housing Units
	Total	Singapore Residents	Non-Residents	Total	Singapore Residents	Non-Residents	Available Units^	Annual Difference	Available Units^	Annual Difference	Available Units#	Annual Difference	Annual Difference
2000	4,027.9	3,273.4	754.5	69.2	43.7	25.5	190,190	10,896	3,480	1,884	828,148	32,327	45,107
2001	4,138.0	3,325.9	812.1	110.1	52.5	57.6	194,984	4,794	6,788	3,308	849,422	21,274	29,376
2002	4,176.0	3,382.9	793.0	37.9	57.0	(19.1)	201,776	6,792	6,788	0	862,198	12,776	19,568
2003	4,114.8	3,366.9	747.9	n.a.*	n.a.*	(45.1)	207,857	6,081	7,536	748	868,774	6,576	13,405
2004	4,166.7	3,413.3	753.4	51.8	46.4	5.5	216,787	8,930	8,168	632	875,887	7,113	16,675
2005	4,265.8	3,457.8	797.9	99.1	54.5	44.5	225,432	8,645	9,527	1,359	879,566	3,679	13,683
2006	4,401.4	3,525.9	875.5	135.6	58.1	77.6	230,752	5,320	9,527	0	879,092	(474)	4,846
2007	4,588.6	3,583.1	1,005.5	187.2	57.2	130.0	233,143	2,391	9,986	459	878,813	(279)	2,571
2008	4,839.4	3,642.7	1,196.7	250.8	59.6	191.2	237,664	4,521	10,430	444	885,140	6,327	11,292
2009	4,987.6	3,733.9	1,253.7	148.2	91.2	57.0	245,864	8,200	10,430	0	883,896	(1,244)	6,956
2010	5,076.7	3,771.7	1,305.0	89.2	37.8	51.3	254,334	8,470	10,430	0	890,212	6,316	14,786
2011	5,183.7	3,789.3	1,394.4	107.0	17.5	89.4	262,162	7,828	10,430	0	901,971	11,759	19,587
2012	5,312.4	3,818.2	1,494.2	128.7	29.0	99.8	273,050	10,888	10,430	0	916,842	14,871	25,759
2013	5,399.2	3,844.8	1,554.4	86.7	26.5	60.2	282,528	9,478	10,430	0	924,729	7,887	17,365
2014	5,469.7	3,870.7	1,599.0	70.6	26.0	44.6	297,998	15,470	13,448	3,018	940,871	16,142	34,630
2015	5,535.0	3,902.7	1,632.3	65.3	32.0	33.3	318,524	20,526	16,904	3,456	968,856	27,985	51,967
2016	5,607.3	3,933.6	1,673.7	72.3	30.9	41.4	338,728	20,204	21,384	4,480	992,472	23,616	48,300
2017	5,612.3	3,965.8	1,646.5	5.0	32.2	(27.3)	356,116	17,388	26,297	4,913	1,017,335	24,863	47,164
2018	5,638.7	3,994.3	1,644.4	26.4	28.5	(2.1)	366,743	10,627	31,566	5,269	1,047,350	30,015	45,911
2019	5,703.6	4,026.2	1,677.4	64.9	31.9	33.0	371,807	5,064	32,925	1,359	1,062,350	15,000	21,423
2020	5,685.8	4,044.2	1,641.6	(17.8)	18.0	(35.8)	374,752	2,945	33,456	531	1,074,667	12,317	15,793

* Point of note: according to the Department of Statistics the "Resident population data for 2003 to 2007 were revised with effect from February 2008 to exclude Singapore residents (citizens and permanent residents) who have been away from Singapore for a continuous period of 12 months or longer as at the reference period. The population data prior to 2003 were not revised. Therefore, the annual difference for 2003 cannot be obtained by subtracting the unrevised 2002 figures from the revised 2003 figures, as reported in Table 1." For this reason, the population decline figure here refer only to the non-resident population which includes holders of permits and employment passes.

includes rental flats managed by HDB. Figures obtained from HDB Annual Reports for years ending 31 March.

^ based on URA quarterly reports for 2nd Quarter of each year, in line with population estimates as at 30 June. EC figures for 1999 and 2000 are estimated.

Source: Singstat, URA, HDB, International Property Advisor

As for those who believe that "when we open our doors, they will flood in", consider the quality of people who "will flood in" if we are not able to create sufficient high value jobs. One last reference for the residential segment: many senior ministers and government officials have recently reiterated that Singapore has no population target. With local unemployment at an 11-year high, technology disrupting jobs and work-from-oversea-homes arrangements, we are likely to see population declines rather than growth.

Fig. 2 shows that the number of pass holders, i.e. tenants renting flats and apartments, declined in the last three out of four years. In the last four years, the overall drop in number of pass holders was about 30,000. However, the total stock of residential units increased by 130,000. As of 31 December 2020, the number of vacant private residential units is 26,394, representing a vacancy rate of 7.0%. Will there be tenants to fill up the apartments if jobs growth remains weak and the utmost priority is for getting more citizens employed?

Industrial segment

The industrial segment is more complex than the other segments discussed above. It is also less understood by general real estate investors. This segment totals more than 530 million sqft and about 54 million sqft, about 10%, are sitting vacant. More than 50 million sqft are under construction and should be completed by 2023. VivoCity has about 1.1 million sqft of lettable area. So if you can imagine 50 vacant VivoCity's worth of industrial space, it will give you an idea of how much non-productive assets lay idle.

Official classification by Jurong Town Corporation splits this segment into: Multiple User Factory (usually strata-titled with many owners and many tenants), Single User Factory (one owner and one tenant), Business Park (similar to offices but limited to "production" type uses) and Warehouse (for storage and logistics). It is important to recognise that these categorisations overlap, e.g. factory space may also be competing for warehouse and logistics users. Large data centres could be classified either as Single User Factory or Business Park.

Well before the pandemic, the industrial segment was already split between assets that perform and assets that struggle with high vacancies. Not much in between.

The pandemic has improved the performance of logistics assets due to ecommerce and factory assets (especially for advanced manufacturing and pharmaceuticals). Work from home and study from home drove up the demand for online applications, and the valuations for data centres surged. On the other hand, some factories suffered. For example, with less vehicular traffic, demand for vehicle maintenance and repairs are down and with less corporate events, the central kitchens for many caterers are struggling.

Post-Covid-19, the split between profitable and struggling industrial properties will widen. For individual investors who own strata-titled industrial units, I would advise you to "cut losses" as the road to rental recovery might take many more years while in the meantime, the 30-year and 60-year leases keep depreciating away.

Healthcare segment
This segment has a bright outlook for investors who are able to get access to large healthcare assets such as bioscience parks, hospitals and healthcare facilities. After global lockdowns ease off, the large numbers of elective surgeries which were postponed should fully resume in the next two years although healthcare tourism might take a few more years to recover. However, healthcare real estate mentioned above are generally not accessible to real estate investors, except through companies and REITs listed on stock exchanges.

There is one category of healthcare real estate in Singapore which retail investors have been buying into: medical suites. In the last 15 years, several strata-titled commercial buildings have apportioned several floors into "medical suites". These are commercial spaces with specifications and designs that allow for medical use. Owners of these commercial units pay a large premium over the value of office space but are restricted to renting out to tenants who are medical practitioners.

And how many new medical practitioners quit from public healthcare to join private practice every year? How many alternative healthcare practices, such as therapists and Chinese medicine clinics, do we have every year? Most investors, and the property agents who sold these medical suites to them, do not have such data and simply got into this segment to avoid the stamp duties on residential properties.

I cautioned investors in Chapter 27 of my second book *Building Your Real Estate Riches* published in 2013 that it will take 10 years to adsorb the stock of completed and vacant medical suites. I also warned that medical practitioners may retire and young ones could also consider setting up medical practices in HDB shops and office or retail spaces. The situation from 2021 and beyond will remain similarly bleak for owners of medical suites: long vacancies between tenants and low demand in the resale market (even if owners are willing to sell below cost). Unless investors are medical practitioners buying for their own use, I would suggest they invest into healthcare real estate through the stock markets.

What does the future of real estate bring? The world will surely recover from this pandemic. But by then, more than 100 million people would have suffered from bad health caused by the coronavirus, more than 2 million people would have died and hundreds of millions of families would have been affected directly or indirectly.

Everyone who survives may be considered a winner. And being winners, we should celebrate. It would be short-sighted to wish that the wonderful vaccines bring life back to the days prior to 2020. It will be a different world, with different job mix, different work patterns, different education and leisure activities, etc. Lifestyles have changed. Habits have changed. We are more accustomed to surveillance and being monitored, giving away our biometric data in exchange for the freedom to move around.

And if certain types of human activities are changed permanently, the form and the substance of real estate will change too. In this chapter, we have considered how 1. ageing demographics, 2. politics and external environment, 3. combined adoption of new technology, and 4. Covid-19, will force real estate to change. While these observations may be applied across the world, my data references and recommendations for investors are focused on Singapore. I would have a different set of recommendations for say, Tokyo or Sydney.

Expect a lot of changes in the urban landscape in the next two decades. There will be lots of renovations at the neighbourhood, city and country level to adapt and rebuild irrelevant and outdated properties to useful assets. Real estate investors need to smarten up: instead of following the old herd, think about how each segment will evolve before clicking on that e-wallet.

With so much change forced by demographics, policies, technology and the pandemic, those who invest into real estate for passive income will need to discard their old approach.

Henceforth, real estate profits are limited to well-researched and active investor-managers. Let's get woke.

Concept proposal for redevelopment of Paya Lebar Airbase

Fig. 3: The concept plan proposal for Paya Lebar Airbase condensed in one visual plan

Runaway Woods @ Paya Lebar: Living in a Forest

Runaway Woods is inspired by the urgency to reverse today's climate and existential crisis of the human species, thus restoring the balanced coexistence between nature and human beings. By integrating state-of-the-art digital technology, climate-smart innovations, renewable energy, community-centric practices, rewilding and conservation of nature, Runaway Woods offers a holistic environment for the future of living, not just in Singapore but all over the world.

In this parcel, every road is repurposed into a verdant grove, every rooftop is converted into agricultural plots and old buildings are carpeted with lush foliage. Two hundred hectares of the site will be set aside as a permanent nature reserve for the long-term rewilding of indigenous primary forest. The trees cool, oxygenate and filter layers of noise, heat, pollution, giving shelter, shade and structure to liveable spaces, whilst releasing moisture back into the air. The transformation of Paya Lebar Airbase and its surrounding industrial areas will inspire the world to observe, adopt and re-learn how we can Live, Work, Play, Learn, Farm and Heal.

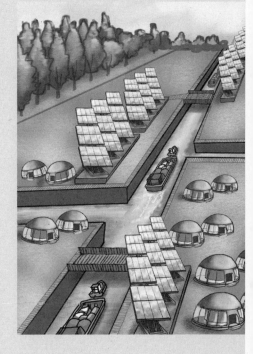

Fig. 4: Canal streets and solar panels line the runways of the airport

Live – Homes are intelligent and tech-infused communities in the Runaway Woods Spiral Residences. They are inspired by China's Hakka Houses, balancing co-living and the nostalgia of kampong dwellings with communal spaces for living, entertainment, kitchen and laundry. The units are designed in an upward spiral with the communal facilities shared by a cluster of units at different elevations. Pedestrian pathways and cycling tracks intertwine residential spaces as most food, medicine and necessities are drone-delivered. Services are localized within the neighbourhood such as 'cloud kitchens' where meals are prepared from kitchens nearest to the customer and communities live zero-waste by minimizing use of disposables and recycling food waste. There will be Service Apartments and Hotels as well, which are self-sustaining in terms of generating their own electricity and harvesting rainwater. (Inspiration: https://www.thecoolist.com/fujian-tulou-chinas-amazing-hakka-houses/)

Fig. 5: Community housing and work spaces

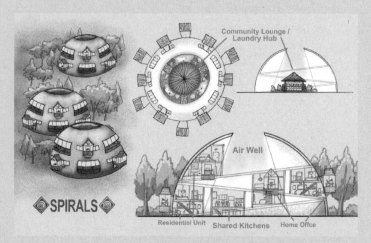

Work – As companies become more decentralized, co-working office spaces can be part of the shared facilities within the Runaway Woods Spiral Residences. They are hybridized social spaces, combining concepts of co-working spaces and 'work-from-home' stations. The Runaway Forest Birdcage Towers would offer tranquil workspaces within a green envelope, where the office experience is more like an outdoor adventure than cubicle life. (Inspiration: https://www.roomsoutdoor.co.uk/)

Fig. 6: Birdcage Towers with homes and offices powered by wind farms

Play – The ubiquitous greenery and thematic structures (like the windmills and birdcages) provide ample opportunities for spontaneous and structured play, thus promoting multi-generational health and wellness. Mini integrated playgrounds will be located at multiple nodes and along jogging paths and cycle tracks within Runaway Woods. The Lakeside Treehouses can tap on technology to enhance the visitor experience, such as the use of augmented reality for visitors to immerse in and experience how the precinct has changed over the decades. (Inspiration: https://www.campadventure.dk/en/)

Learn – The Runaway Woods Academy offers outdoor and experiential education for young and old, inspired by Green School Bali. The various facilities and activities at Runaway Woods – such as farming, forest walks, renewable energy, reservoir lake, rewilded primary forest – would serve as the Academy's extended campus, providing students with hands-on, practical and ecology-centric short and long courses. Local and international conservationists and sustainability experts can serve as visiting faculty. (Inspiration: https://waldorfgarden.org , www.greenschool.org)

Farm – Agriculture 4.0 using robots would drive crop yields and operational efficiency, such as in the Runaway Woods Hangar Farms, which are repurposed indoor vertical farms. Agro-ecological methods (i.e. the science of managing farms as ecosystems) such as crop rotation and agroforestry practices will be adopted to minimize environmental impact. (Inspiration: https://www.vox.com/energy-and-environment/2017/11/8/16611710/vertical-farms)

Fig. 8: Learning to go back to basics in the midst of nature

Fig. 9: Aircraft hangars converted into farms, processing factories and logistics facilities

Heal – Globally benchmarked assisted living and healthcare best practices in Runaway Woods offer best care for multi-generational families while being in a homely environment within Nature. The

Bamboo Healing Huts are nestled amidst thick bamboo growth to provide shade and quiet respite, giving a boost to visitor wellness, and are tech-infused to provide 24/7 monitoring systems, backed by certified care partners for support. (Inspiration: https://www. mygreenpod.com/articles/forest-bathing/)

Fig. 10: Bamboo healing forest surround healthcare and recuperation facilities

2. The New Tech — New Jobs Disconnect

First published on Storm-Asia.com, 12 April 2018

Jon Ang worked in a major bank for most of his working life. Until he was let go at the age of 45. With a degree in Business and Finance and an inclination for technology and data processing, Jon was the bridge between the back offices of the Finance Division and the IT department. The adoption of more efficient and streamlined payment processes made possible by innovative FinTech applications meant that fewer workers were needed in the Finance Division. Jon and a few of his colleagues engineered their own redundancy.

But, the bank was compassionate. In addition to the severance package, Jon was given opportunities to sign up for several skills-related courses for free. After a certificate course, he took up a diploma programme, all the while applying for jobs in the industry.

But his work experience was becoming more irrelevant by the day, and after one year, he started his own company as a career counsellor providing job search services for retrenched bankers.

Or should he have become a Grab driver?

This is a common story in a society that wants to reach for the brightest stars that technology has to offer. It's something that needs to be done, but there will be casualties in its wake.

It is impossible for anyone keeping up with business and market news online to miss the advertisements and loud proclamations about the multitude of companies embracing FinTech, PropTech, EdTech, Cypto-currencies, Blockchain technology, Artificial Intelligence and Big Data.

Finance industry leaders have expressed confidence that Singapore's banks will continue to grow in this new epoch of technology disruptions.

Head in the sand

Economists are of the opinion that higher productivity from the latest technologies and innovations will lead to more jobs being created, as has happened in previous industrial revolutions.

Even university professors leading the charge in disruptive technologies are optimistic that more high-value jobs will spawn out of the repetitive jobs that will be displaced by automation.

I have had conversations with government officials who are optimistic about the abundance of high-value jobs created by robots and artificial intelligence. They do, however, lament the limited supply of skilled labour.

I asked the bankers, "How many bank branches might be closed with the banks' adoption of mobile wallets, FinTech, Blockchain and Big Data? How many jobs in the banks' middle and back offices will be redundant?" No answers are forthcoming.

I asked the policy makers and technology creators, "A hundred engineering jobs were created which subsequently led to the retirement of a thousand taxi drivers, do you really think there will be a net gain in jobs?" They firmly believe that they are correct.

I asked the economists, "The correlation between population, labour force and GDP worked well in the agriculture and manufacturing economies. But in this tech-disrupted economy or going forward into the 4th Industrial Revolution, would such a model remain valid?"

The economists are sticking to their methods. They are happy to forecast GDP growth, by relying on age-old and tested economic constructs of labour force growth, labour productivity and total factor productivity.

The stark reality

Where are the net additional jobs created from tech disruptions? Does it count that we needed to employ a few hundred bicycle marshals across Singapore to pick up strewn bicycles? That job exists to put right our lack of civic-mindedness, it is not a job created out of technology and lifestyle changes.

GDP GROWTH

Year	2014	2015	2016	2017
GDP at 2010 prices (S$mill)	389,637.4	398,369.4	407,918.4	422,679.1
Annual GDP growth		2.24%	2.40%	3.62%
GDP growth 2017 over 2014				8.48%

Source: IPA, Singstat

The Singapore economy did well to maintain relevance by keeping up with automation and transforming our industries by embracing disruptive technologies. Over the last three years, adoption of new technologies in manufacturing and services industries and a strong global market led to an 8.5% growth in Gross Domestic Product between 2017 and 2014.

However, total employment grew by a mere 0.6% over the same period.

TOTAL EMPLOYMENT

Year	2014	2015	2016	2017
Total employment excluding Foreign Domestic Workers	3,401,500	3,424,800	3,433,400	3,422,700
Annual change in total employment		23,300	8,600	-10,700
Employment growth 2017 over 2014				0.62%

Source: IPA, Singstat

In fact, as the Singapore economy becomes more tech-enabled, the total number of jobs available will shrink further.

This is consistent with the population data from Singstat, which shows that for the 12-month period to June 2017, the number of foreigners with work passes dropped by 36,000.

During that period, the total population of Singapore grew by a mere 5,000 people, far below the annual target of about 70,000 to 80,000 that will take us to the 6.9 million population in 2030.

The disturbing disconnect

"The disconnect between a rising GDP and diminishing jobs is becoming so pronounced that it's difficult to continue to ignore it, although I'm still somewhat amazed at how few economists, even at this stage, are willing to step forward and finally acknowledge that the underlying assumption of classical economic theory — that productivity creates more jobs than it replaces — is no longer credible." — **Jeremy Rifkin, The Zero Marginal Cost Society (2014)**

Global management consultant Bain & Company published a report in February 2018 titled *Labor 2030: The Collision of Demographics,*

Automation and Inequality. They did not sugar coat their findings. In the second paragraph of the Executive Summary, Bain stated that before the year 2030, automation could make 20% to 25% of the current jobs in the USA irrelevant, "hitting middle- to low-income workers the hardest".

Bain & Company is just one of the hundreds of multi-national corporations warning about the rapid decline of jobs due to disruptive technologies. Forward-thinking industrialists such as Tesla CEO Elon Musk and Virgin founder Richard Branson are already calling for Universal Basic Income to support the long-term unemployed and the unemployable.

Sadly, these are not topics that the local media are keen on pursuing. The Singapore government's stance may be a preference for presenting positive news to the citizens so that we do not face the painful hard truths.

3. Technology — Boon to Singapore, Bane of Property Professionals

Co-authored with Justin Chong; first published on Storm-Asia.com, 12 June 2018

The flip side to technology could have a significant effect in the property industry.

It is estimated that technology could result in the loss of anywhere from $15 million to $30 million worth of legal fees and over $100 million worth of agency commissions annually. Not to mention job losses in the thousands among property agents.

The Real Estate Industry Transformation Map (ITM) was announced by Dr Koh Poh Koon, then Minister of State for National Development at his ministry's Committee of Supply debate in March 2017. In support of the ITM, HDB streamlined the resale transaction process and introduced a new HDB Resale Portal.

The powerful system allows people to check on their eligibility to sell or buy a flat, halve the transaction process to 8 weeks, and reduce the number of appointments with HDB to just one. The bulk of transactions will not require a valuation report to be provided by a third-party valuation firm.

The largest property trading portal

With over one million HDB flats and over three million occupiers in total, the HDB Resale Portal will be one of the largest property trading portals in the world!

Every year, more than 20,000 resale transactions and over 30,000 rental transactions may be put through this system.

And if we add on new technologies such as e-contracts, blockchain and big data, we will have a property portal that can provide buyers, sellers, tenants and sub-tenants with fuss-free resale and rental transactions. Bank loans could also be integrated into the system via e-contracts, simplifying the process further.

This could all be a part of creating a "future-ready real estate sector that will continue to provide good jobs for Singaporeans" as announced by Dr Koh.

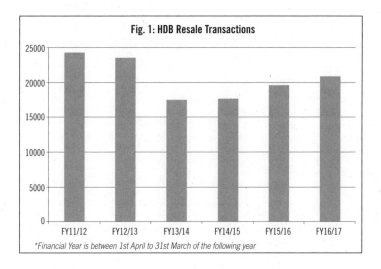

Fig. 1: HDB Resale Transactions

*Financial Year is between 1st April to 31st March of the following year

Jobs will be lost

With such a powerful portal, we foresee four areas where businesses will be impacted by this efficient system.

1. No valuation report

As it stands, the new procedures have reduced the need for external valuation reports. We estimate that about 80% of the annual 20,000 resale transactions will not require an external valuation report. This saves time and cost for the resale participants. It also removes about 16,000 cases from the valuers' desks. For the qualified valuers, our guess is that about 50 jobs may have to be reconfigured, i.e. they will have to work on other real estate segments such as private residences and industrial properties, or expand their capabilities to include tax valuation and consultancy.

2. No lawyers needed

Since HDB is the owner of the flats, "sellers" are merely transferring the long-term leases to the "buyers" through HDB's website in "resale" transactions. About 90% of these transactions are normal transactions which do not involve court orders, such as in divorce or inheritance cases. We estimate that for 90% of resale transactions, lawyers would not be needed to represent the parties involved especially if bank loans were seamlessly integrated into the portal. Based on checks with lawyers, about 50 lawyers' jobs could be reorganised with less conveyancing work for HDB transactions.

3. Greater transparency

With the infrastructure in place for this portal, it is fairly easy for HDB to allow all "buyers" and "sellers" who have registered their intent to transact to see each other. The flats of all the qualified and eligible "sellers", their flats' selected photographs, location and asking prices could be displayed on the portal for all qualified and eligible "buyers" to view. The information displayed on this portal would have much better integrity than independent property portals as it would only contain listings of flats for sale after the "sellers" have been confirmed as eligible by HDB. When the HDB Resale Portal becomes a listing portal, we estimate that the number of HDB listings in newspapers and independent property portals will reduce by up to 90% from today.

4. DIY transactions

"Buyers" and "sellers" will logically adopt the DIY service model that immediately eliminates the need for estate agents. Eligible "buyers" and "sellers", both pre-qualified by HDB, meet online and exchange viewing schedules, then negotiate and settle on a price and click through to the final steps to obtain HDB's approval for the resale transaction.

What will be the relevance of estate agents when the owner of this portal is also the approving authority and the owner of the flat? The portal would perform the role of an agent with greater transparency, efficiency and without listing costs and commissions! How many property agents could possibly lose their jobs?

We estimate that as much as 80% (or 16,715) of the resale transactions will eventually be completed directly without any property agents involved. Only about 20% or 4,000 transactions annually would require property agents to serve either the "sellers" and/or the "buyers".

The main reasons that these transactions require the services of property agents are family issues, language and education issues and insufficient time for self-service.

Currently, about 15,000 out of the 30,000 property agents are involved in HDB resale and HDB rentals.

When HDB Resale Portal allows "buyers" and "sellers" to see each other for DIY transactions, up to 10,000 agents' jobs will be affected. Of these, 5,000 might leave the industry altogether. The other half will have to move to other segments such as industrial or commercial properties or expand into international property sales.

As the average total commission per transaction of a $400,000 resale HDB flat is around 2% for both "buyers" and "sellers", the 16,715 cases taking the DIY route would reduce industry commissions by about $128 million per year.

Other services added

As Singapore presses ahead with automation of processes for greater efficiency, you could see municipal services, utilities and a whole array of e-commerce services being added onto the list, and private residential properties could be transacted through a sister portal.

Such technological disruptions and transformations will continue to gain traction, bringing lots of convenience to all households in the Smart Nation.

Some property agents who are looking at the horizon, are already consolidating and looking for public funding through IPOs. Generally, property agents and conveyancing lawyers should brace themselves for the impact to come.

4. Total Defence Should Include Food Security

With additional research and reporting by Yeoh Theng; first published on Storm-Asia. com, 8 June 2020

Beefing up on food security is similar to building up more healthcare capacity and hospitals. With the population tree enlarging its canopy, this rapidly ageing country needs more hospitals and a more robust and comprehensive healthcare system, including an urgent development in healthcare manpower.

But we have dragged our feet on both food security and increasing healthcare capacity for decades. Every country recognises the need to have secure sources of food supply, including stockpiling essential food items unilaterally or in cooperation with neighbouring countries.

In this regard, Singapore signed an Agreement on the ASEAN Food Security Reserve which included the ASEAN Emergency Rice Reserve in October 1979. It was significant enough that then Prime Minister Lee Kuan Yew noted the signing of the agreement in a speech when he opened the 15th ASEAN Ministerial Meeting on 14 June 1982.

Despite the early recognition of food security and signing the ASEAN agreement, farming and agricultural activities in Singapore declined from the 1980s as economic growth took precedence over food security.

With abundant and cheap food sources around the world, coupled with strong logistics and good quality food packaging, it remains cheaper for Singapore to import food. Meanwhile we generated more economic value and profits through rezoning agricultural land into "higher value" uses, such as by increasing the intensity of land use through higher plot ratios and selling residential strata titles in the air.

Self-production of food was hardly profitable and never deemed a high priority in land-scarce Singapore.

However, the conversation about food security never ceased. We are regularly reminded that we need to improve our self-sufficiency in food production by episodes of food disruptions such as mad cow disease, bird flu, red tide, swine flu and natural disasters.

Realistic goal?

40 years on, in March 2019, Minister for Environment and Water Resources Masagos Zulkifli announced an ambitious "30 by 30" target: that we will self-produce 30% of our food requirements by the year 2030.

But questions remain about how we might achieve 30% self-sufficiency when, for the last few decades, we have depended on about 170 countries for 90% of our food supply.

We need to quickly build sufficient manpower and know-how for the production, packing and distribution of vegetables, eggs and fish.

On the economic front, our small consumer market and limited production volumes, coupled with high cost of land and labour could mean that consumers may find local greens and meats to be poorer value-for-money as compared to the price of imported foods.

Singapore is ranked by the Economist Intelligence Unit as the No.1 country in food security primarily by keeping food prices affordable and maintaining high standards for food hygiene supported by Singapore's extensive logistics network.[1]

As pointed out by renowned food security researchers Professor Paul Teng and Jose Montesclaros from the Centre for Non-Traditional Security Studies at the Nanyang Technological University's S. Rajaratnam School of International Studies, the reality for Singapore in year 2030 is that:

"The handful of self-produced food items will likely remain a handful, for reasons of no comparative advantage to produce food that requires large tracts of land and special growing conditions. But a 30% self-production in at least three strategic food items will give Singapore some buffer should there be short-term supply disruptions.

"The added value of fostering a new sub-sector of supporting companies could also lead to more economic opportunities for agritech innovations. To meet the remaining 70% of food needs will still require that the country pays attention to developments overseas and plays its role as a responsible global citizen in efforts at addressing food security elsewhere."

COVID-19 made our need for food security even more urgent. On 8 April, two months after declaring DORSCON (Disease Outbreak

---

1 *Global Food Security Index*, The Economist Intelligence Unit, https://foodsecurityindex.eiu.com/Country

Response System Condition) Orange — the second-highest alert level — and at the start of the Circuit Breaker, the Singapore Food Authority (SFA) announced a S$30 million grant to assist the agri-food industry to "accelerate the ramping up" of local production of eggs, leafy vegetables and fish.

This was followed by SFA calling for a tender to rent nine farm sites on 12 May. These vegetable farms are situated on the rooftops of multi-storey car parks in Housing & Development Board (HDB) estates. Those who are successful in their tenders will sign a three-year tenancy agreement to build and operate the farms.

Who would risk it?

The three-year lease period includes the time required to set up the high-density farming system and the production, storage and packing system, as well as the time required to strip the system apart at the end of the lease.

The planting and harvesting period could be less than 33 months.

Farmers keen to bid for these car park rooftop sites have to undertake financial risks and invest in equipment, manpower and supply chain systems.

Would these carpark rooftop farms be economically viable when a key element of the tender is the rent bidders propose to pay?

The HDB manages more than 2,100 car parks and over 1,000 of them are multi-storey car parks. The popularity and convenience of on-demand taxi services such as Grab and Gojek point to a gradual reduction in car ownership and therefore, the utilisation of car parks will be reduced.

With rooftops being exposed to the heat and rain, we can guess that they will remain largely vacant.

Given that these farmers will be providing a much-needed service to boost the country's self-sufficiency in food, must rentals be charged on the abundant and underutilised real estate on the top floors of multi-storey car parks?

If we were genuinely serious about food security, shouldn't we provide the rooftops free of rent to the farmers who are risking capital to enhance food sufficiency for the population?

Rubbing salt

The policy makers' intentions to enhance food sufficiency also seem to contradict their actions.

The third-generation Oh' Farms will be closed for business at the end of June 2020 as the farmland has to be returned to the Singapore Land Authority. Oh' Farms comprises 220 tropical greenhouses spread over 262,000 sqft (about 4 football fields). Oh is unable to continue his agriculture business and is in fact looking for ways to pay for the reinstatement of the farm back to grassland to return to the State.

At the same time, Singapore has opened the market to import poultry and eggs from Poland. Does the cost of airfreighting fresh eggs make better economic sense than boosting egg production in Singapore?

While we do not produce enough eggs locally to feed our demand of 3 to 5 million eggs daily, Singapore does not consume all the eggs ithat are available. Would a better management of local resources be a solution to consider?

In defence of food

In order to ensure that the "30 by 30" target will be reached and surpassed, policy planners might consider amending the way government budgets are allocated and how Key Performance Indicators (KPIs) are measured.

If food security is accorded the same level of importance as national security, perhaps the budget to develop food self-sufficiency and high-tech farming could come under the Ministry of Defence (MINDEF) and the Ministry of Home Affairs.

Supporting this idea, fourth-generation farmer Kenny Eng, believes that food security is sufficiently important that farming activities should be included as part of National Service. A meaningful period of time during a national serviceman's training stint should be allocated to learning about various aspects of farming, the Director of Nyee Phoe Group emphasised.

MINDEF is already contributing to Singapore's environmental sustainability through green buildings, hybrid vehicles, food waste management and solar energy in 12 Singapore Armed Forces (SAF) camps by March 2021. Such involvement in green initiatives presents an opportunity to incorporate local capabilities such as farming within our SAF army camps to enhance the nation's food security.

All SAF and Singapore Civil Defence Force (SCDF) camps that undertake basic military training could allocate 5,000 sqft of outdoor space and/or 2,000 sqft for indoor farming. Soldiers may be rostered for farming duties, learning about various methods of cultivating and harvesting leafy vegetables, roots, stems, fruits and herbs. Some camps may accommodate fish farming, too.

Proper planning and integration of soldiers' training schedules with the lifecycle management of crops can lead to a more productive and efficient use of resources. Whether during peacetime or an emergency, SAF and SCDF camps have the resources and know-how to support the nation's food production.

This could potentially lead to jobs in agriculture, if the 2030 self-sufficiency vision is realised.

Teaching everyone

Expanding on this line of thought, Food Security should be included as the seventh pillar of the Total Defence strategy. We should instil an appreciation for food production and awareness about food security for students starting from pre-school and kindergarten levels. Students in primary and secondary schools should be given practical hands-on lessons about various methods of farming vegetables.

The Ministry of Education (MOE) should allocate an annual budget to provide every primary and secondary school student with at least 30 hours for farming activities and related lessons every academic year. Each school may set aside about 1,000 sqft of outdoor space for farming and one classroom as an agri-lab or an indoor farm. Students should be rostered to tend to the crops, and also go on field trips to farms here and in the region.

Several dozen schools have been closed in the last decade, and most of the school buildings and compounds have been left fallow. MOE could convert one vacant school compound within each school-zone into a horticulture lab and activity centre for students to be further immersed in farming technology and agricultural sciences. Such conversions to re-position the abandoned school compounds to agriculture education use will also contribute to reducing our carbon footprint.

It is not sufficient to merely allocate budgets to MINDEF and MOE, we need to set longer term milestones that will take Singapore beyond the "30 by 30" goals, such as achieving 70% self-sufficiency by the year 2040 and 100% by 2050.

With 30 years of investments in educating students and training National Servicemen to farm, supported by new technologies, we should be confident of meeting our food security goals by 2050.

Today's fight

Allocating a long-term budget to MINDEF and MOE for the purpose of security is no different from allocating S$100 billion[2] to fight climate change over the next 50 to 100 years.

Speaking at the National Day Rally 2019, Prime Minister Lee Hsien Loong highlighted the need to prepare for the negative impact of climate change.

"Climate change defences should be treated with utmost seriousness, just like the Singapore Armed Forces (SAF)," he said, and added that we need to "work steadily at it, maintain a stable budget year after year, keep your eye on the target and do it over many years and several generations."

Well, climate change is a 50- to 100-year challenge and we have already started preparing in earnest.

Meanwhile, COVID-19 is forcing us to stare food security issues squarely in the face. Shouldn't we urgently take action on food security with "utmost seriousness", too?

---

2 "NDR 2019: It could cost S$100 billion or more to protect Singapore against rising sea levels, PM Lee says", ChannelNewsAsia, 18 Aug 2019, https://www.channel-newsasia.com/news/singapore/ndr-2019-singapore-climate-change-costs-rising-sea-levels-11819402

5. Imagining Our New Smart City with Bold Urban Planning

Co-authored with Tay Kheng Soon and Yeoh Lam Keong

Founding Prime Minister Lee Kuan Yew once said that Singapore has to be constantly building and rebuilding itself. He was very right! A thriving small island city state has no choice but to regularly upgrade its infrastructure and its living and working environment to remain relevant.

This is not only necessary, but it is also possible in Singapore because the State owns more than 80% of all the land which it leases out according to a master plan. As buildings age or become obsolete, they are rebuilt to new standards and with greater sophistication. To anticipate and regulate development and redevelopment, Singapore has a master plan that is reviewed and revised periodically.

The planning ideas and methodology have tended to be adapted from the planning methodologies developed in Britain, Australia and the United States. The 1947 Town and Country Planning Act of Britain forms the conceptual basis of the Singapore Planning

Act modified to serve our needs over the years. Thus evolved land-use planning as an essentially two-dimensional method.

What we call 2D planning is the standard planning method used everywhere including in Singapore. It is primarily based on allocating land, its use and its plot ratios. This is to achieve orderly development of the whole island. But now that most of Singapore's land is developed, we need a new planning method as we build and rebuild.

This is what we call 3D planning, based on the total volume of necessary space each person needs in a high performing economy, grossed up over the entire population. Once the total is known, a merge between new building morphologies (more simply, design structure and arrangement) with new land parcellation can come together. In 2D planning, this is difficult because the processes of land use allocation is distinct from innovative building morphology. Necessary spatial innovation is thus constrained.

From 2D to 3D

With 3D planning, we can actually use less land surface by innovating multipurpose linked and stacked building forms like that in Kampong Admiralty and Tampines Hub. This way, we economise on land, reduce the need to travel, increase liveability and social and environmental synergy. For example, densities in the south of Singapore can be very high, medium in the middle and very low density in the north as we build and rebuild over the next 50 years.

Prof. Tay Kheng Soon adapted the 3D method from the research done by Cambridge University's Centre for Land Use and Built-form Studies published in its two books, *The Geometry of Environment* (1971) and *Urban Space and Structures* (1972). Conservatism

prevented these ideas from entering the town planning and urban development mainstream.

Singapore became a hugely successful and liveable city, but times have changed. Singapore is at an inflection point where we have both a pressing need and an opportunity to remake our urban landscape for a new phase of development.

The old model of land use planning allowed us to build industrial estates for labour intensive industries and surround them with affordable housing units for the masses. This was Singapore's first stage of economic development. Traditional land use planning also helped Singapore move to the next stage of development, to become a higher value-added economy. In this new phase, we went on to develop purpose-built industrial buildings, state-of-the-art commercial centres, and high-quality public housing. Much attention was also paid to designing sustainable, pleasing public spaces including building a network of park connectors. However, we are now being eclipsed by regional competitors, who are also moving up the higher value-added economy chain.

To transit to the third stage of a knowledge-intensive economy, we need 3D planning. For example, the knowledge-intensive economy requires greater spatial integration of educational systems, especially centres of higher learning with R&D and commercial or industrial activities. Another example is that a much higher density of communication between businesses, innovators, R&D, and customers is facilitated by 3D planning.

Ageing leases present an opportunity for renewal

Another pressing reason for change is the asset erosion of Housing Board (HDB) flats as their 99-year leases run down. As of 2020, more than 200,000 flats are above 40 years of age (almost 20% of total stock of 1.06 million flats). In 10 years, more than 200,000 flats will be more than 50 years old, while more than 500,000 flats will be more than 40 years old (about 40% of total stock of an expected 1.20 million HDB flats). As many HDB flats near the second half of their 99-year leases, they will need to be refreshed or redeveloped. Reinforced concrete buildings are designed for a 100-year lifespan. This means a 50-100 year time cycle of adaptation and re-building is needed. The mass ageing cycle of HDB estates present land planners with an opportunity to think out of the box and to design whole estates for the future.

This is not easy. Redesigning new building morphology and intensification of land use have to be done in tandem with what the work force of the future and their families need. A whole-of-society effort is thus required.

Rebuilding all HDB estates en bloc at government cost, after affordably renewing the leases, will enable this comprehensive urban redesign of the new knowledge economy, in a way that secures the needed political cooperation of all citizens.

A vision of the future

What would a 3D-planned township look like? Imagine living in high-rise residential towers on top of an interconnected multifunction

podium that houses schools, offices, robotic factories, social and commercial and recreational facilities on the lower floors. The need to travel is greatly reduced. Advanced technology integrates work and learning for everyone. The entire green roof deck of the podium becomes a large traffic-free park for kindergartens, families and neighbours. Large extended solar panels overhead keep the place cool yet generate energy for the large in-door farms in the podium.

Plot ratios of 5:1 or higher, through stacked 3D design actually reduce building footprint and release more open spaces. Current HDB ratios are about 2.5:1, so 3D planning will result in twice the floor space for a given land area, increasing land use efficiency and adequacy, even with a significantly larger population. Reduced need to travel further reduce roads. The interconnected podium links the entire island and turns it into a campus-like city.

This is in fact the value-creation environment for the new knowledge economy. It enables everyone to fit into this concept. Imagine one million new higher education students from the best and brightest in Asia living and learning here with our own students. Living and learning together, life-long friendships formed will naturally result in economic and cultural ties throughout the region and further afield. This is Singapore's future!

On a ratio of six students to one tutor, there will be jobs for 170,000 tutors, 17,000 administrative staff. A local bed and breakfast economy, restaurants, provision for recreation, laundry, housekeeping, logistics, and the arts. In other words, jobs for everyone. It's a whole new local and regional economy. Singapore can take inspiration from Boston, which has 35 universities and colleges, and is the most prominent centre of learning in the world.

At the macro level, the optimal configuration of commuting, logistics and transport between residential, industrial, commercial and research and education activities linked by state-of-art ICT connectivity will mean a smart city with a higher level of productivity, and competitiveness as well as environmental sustainability. Innovation and creativity will also flourish from optimum network externalities. Singapore will then be the only country in which 80% of its labour force lives in a new super productive yet beautiful and state-of-the-art residence with tremendous conviviality, buzz and vitality.

Such a vision is only possible because the 50-100 year HDB lease extension and rebuilding cycle which we recommend as the first two key parts of our public housing reforms. It will require a strategic 50-100 year comprehensive land use master plan. The 3D planning method integrates all the abovementioned social, economic, political, and environmental factors.

But to imagine we can shift 80% of the population into this dream city without affordable lease extension and rebuilding, new ownership housing priced at cost, as well as adequate access to subsidized rental housing recommended in our proposals, is politically naive and unrealistic.

The lessons of the political turmoil in the US, UK or HK is that because of the lack of sufficient social protection and stake in the economy, political legitimacy and stability is fragile and could easily be the victim of progress, if social well-being and the social compact is not sufficiently safeguarded.

PART 2

PUBLIC HOUSING

6. Reflecting on the HDB Issue – My Journey

Many long-time followers of my commentaries would remember that I crossed swords with the authorities about the issue of HDB "ownership" and the decaying value of old flats. This chapter chronicles my journey of research in the public housing sector over the last 10 years and how my worries remain for more than 500,000 families whose flats are more than 40 years old by the year 2030.

My first major HDB write-up

It was in the second half of 2012 that I became more involved in public housing research. Before that I tracked public housing data to better understand the total residential supply, demand, rentals and investments, etc.

I started looking wider into issues around public housing such as affordability, lease decay and value decline as well as how these issues eat away at CPF monies and affect the retirement adequacy of HDB dwellers. When I put all the information together and add the realisation that HDB dwellers make up 80% of Singapore's resident households, I started to worry.

In April 2013, I wrote a long discourse on "Re-examining the basis for public housing – shelter or asset?" and the Institute of Policy Studies (IPS), a think-tank at Lee Kuan Yew School of Public Policy, National University of Singapore, published it on their communications platform IPS Commons. Reference: https://ipscommons.sg/re-examining-the-basis-for-public-housing-shelter-or-asset/

I suggested why HDB resale prices were becoming less affordable and I pointed out a few challenges that required urgent attention: the slow pace of construction, the need to educate the public about HDB's role in public housing, and clearing up the market confusion between cooling measures versus making housing policies more attractive.

In this opinion piece, I included 4 proposals about how HDB could go "back to basics" instead of trying to be "many things to many people":

a. HDB to be a market maker, buying back resale flats at a price formula pegged to inflation and GDP growth and reselling them after renovations
b. the value of new subsidised flats must not exceed four times the couple's joint annual income
c. revert to the original intent of HDB to provide shelter instead of introducing patchwork of rules to prevent overheating in the market
d. provide more rental flats for the disadvantaged and the senior citizens

The article was subsequently republished as Chapter 7 in my third book *Real Estate Realities* in 2014.

Since then, the HDB has slowly increased its stock of rental flats from 52,000 to about 63,000 units (or 5% of total stock) to shelter the poor and disadvantaged. However, the labyrinth of policies has become more complex and prices of new flats continue to be expensive for young home buyers because they remain pegged at a discount to resale prices, which have not dropped especially in matured estates.

I am not sure what to read of the policy maker's declarations to price new flats at affordable levels. On the one hand, incomes of recent graduates I taught in Ngee Ann Polytechnic and the universities are not rising. On the other hand, new launches in popular estates such as Bidadari (classified under Toa Payoh), Bishan, Kallang and Queenstown where resale prices remain high, are very expensive because they are priced at a discount to still-high resale prices. HDB priced new 4-room flats of about 1,000 sqft in Bishan at over $600,000. That level of pricing limits the market to young couples from higher income families. Couples from poorer families will either "self-select" themselves out of these unaffordable new flats, or worse, stretch their finances to the limit in the hope that their careers will be high-flying and they can resell the Bishan flats for a windfall in 10 years' time.

In 2015 and 2016 I continued to caution the market about the untenable excess in housing supply and the risks of high homeownership rates against the depreciating values of old flats. However, the market remained upbeat with increasing numbers of million-dollar flats transacted. Some of the priciest flats are more than 40 years old, such as those in Tiong Bahru or Marine Parade. Some buyers of high-priced old flats were probably betting that the government will extend the benefits of SERS (Selective En bloc Redevelopment Scheme) to all the old HDB flats.

In March 2017, National Development Minister Lawrence Wong sounded a caution to such exuberance in a post on the MND blog (https://mndsingapore.wordpress.com/2017/03/). He reminded the public that "only 4% of HDB flats have been identified for SERS since it was launched in 1995" and that the government will continue to maintain a strict set of selection criteria for SERS. He said:

> "...for the vast majority of HDB flats, the leases will eventually run out, and the flats will be returned to HDB, who will in turn have to surrender the land to the State. As the leases run down, especially towards the tail-end, the flat prices will come down correspondingly."

I was delighted that Minister Lawrence Wong advised the public to be more level-headed and realistic. Afterall Singaporeans have always had odd expectations about how the government will, without fail, swoop in to save us from our bad fortunes. Singaporeans who have "purchased" HDB flats have signed an Agreement for Lease which stated that the "Lease of the Flat" has a term of 99 years. They also signed a Memorandum of Lease as a Lessee of the flat. The Memorandum of Lease spells out the easement rights and privileges of the Lessee as well as special covenants where the Lessor (i.e. the Housing & Development Board) restricts the Lessee from certain actions such as assigning the rights of the flat to other parties or keeping "any animal bird fish or insect in the Flat". Finally, the third document that they sign is the Lease for the physical property, that is, the flat.

It looks to me like most people have forgotten their lease obligations: 99 years. And that at the end of the lease term, "the flats will be returned to HDB".

Sellers demand unrealistically high prices thinking that SERS is a definite certainty and they are hopeful for regular asset enhancements and upgrading programs. However, if HDB "owners" could keep in mind that every year that passed is equal 1/99 years of lease depreciated, we could be more objective about the value of HDB flats when we resell them in the open market. With more realistic expectations, the constant upward push of resale prices could correct to a gradual downward trend as the total stock of HDB flats become older and older. I would consider the slow value drop reasonable as flat dwellers have "consumed" part of the useful life of the 99-year lease of the flat.

The second and third major pieces

The Minister's blog post generated hundreds of articles in the main stream media and millions of social media comments. Many Singaporeans seemingly felt short-changed having gotten their dream-bubbles burst by the Minister's kind reminder: at the end of 99 years of lease, the flat has to be returned to HDB, with zero value left.

The wake-up call was significant for tens, if not hundreds, of thousands of HDB dwelling families. The shaded part of Fig. 1 refers to the flats completed in the two decades of 1970s and 1980s. As of today in 2021, there are about 550,000 flats with less than 70 years of lease remaining, i.e. they are more than 30 years old. Of these 550,000 flats, more than 200,000 are already past 40 years of age and have less than 60 years of lease left. Note: Those that were built in the 1960s have either been demolished or in the case of Tiong Bahru flats, are under conservation.

Fig. 1: The total number of HDB dwellings completed over the past six decades exceeded 1.2 million units. About 127,000 have been demolished over the years, mostly through the SERS programme. The numbers above include about 8,600 units of flats under the Design, Build and Sell Scheme.

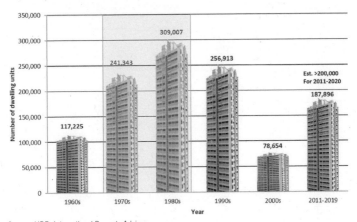

Source: HDB, International Property Advisor

Together with a few bright students from the Department of Real Estate in National University of Singapore, we explored the challenges posed by the ageing HDB flats, how their lease decay and value depreciation will pan out. Responding to an enquiry from *The Straits Times,* Ms Soh Yun Yee and I analysed how the depreciating leases will pan out in future and created an estimate to illustrate how an old, high-priced flat's value will decay as its lease declines to its expiry date. The example was taken off a 5-room flat in Marine Parade that was sold for $860,000 in 2017, with 56 years of lease left. See Fig. 2.

The main factor causing the downward pressure on the value of old flats with short leases is the rapidly shrinking pool of qualified purchasers. The older a flat is, the more restrictions faced by young families in loan financing and use of CPF to pay for the flats.

Fig. 2: How a HDB flat might depreciate in value as its lease declines. This estimate was done based on the financing rules applicable in early 2017. *The Straits Times* **adapted and published this chart on 12 April 2017.**

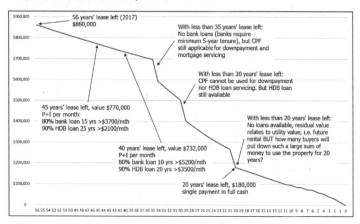

Source: Soh Yun Yee, International Property Advisor

The public perception about value decay is muddled with another value depreciation concept referred to as the Bala's Table. The Bala's Table or the Singapore Land Authority's Leasehold Table is a table of values that compares the value of land with different lease tenures, between freehold and shorter leases such as 99-year, 60-year and 30-year. The Bala's Table does not account for changes in restrictions, such as financing and ownership, as the lease decays.

In 2017 and 2018, I had to respond to several dozen enquiries from the media, industry colleagues and members of the public about these issues.

Ms Jolene Ng Hui Yi, Ms Soh Yun Yee and I also overlayed the HDB lease decay with Singapore's ageing demographics and the increasing number of deaths of home owners. We tried to estimate the impact on the resale value of HDB flats when more and more owners pass away. Statistically speaking, 90% of their surviving children would also own properties and a large proportion would be restricted from inheriting the flats. These beneficiaries will sell the old flats so as to share their inheritance as cash. This growing category of resale flats, mostly older ones in growing numbers, will add to the resale pool of over 20,000 per year.

The research, analysis and forecasts were published as Chapter 1, Nearing the Edge of the Precipice: Ageing Population and the Housing Market, and Chapter 2, Facing the 99-Year Leasehold Chasm of Public Housing, in my fifth book *Preparing for a Property Upturn* published in September 2017.

In that excercise, we estimated that by the year 2031, the number of flats added to the resale pool each year due to the death of the remaining spouse of old flat "owners" whose children are unable to inherit the flats to be at least 8,000 units. This would add about 40% to the volume of roughly 20,000 resale transactions a year. Since 90% of resident households own the residences they live in, the bulk of resale HDB buyers would be relatively young families and some retirees and downgraders who do not mind the shorter leases. By that year 2031, the number of young people in Generation Z who are eligible to purchase HDB flats would be far fewer than the Millennials who are buying flats today. Refer to Fig. 1 on page 22 in Chapter 1 of this book for the various sizes of each age cohort of the population tree.

For this chapter, I updated the research from 2017 by engaging with a team of A+ students from the Singapore Management University. We reviewed the two chapters published in 2017 and drew upon the latest sets of population, households and HDB data to extrapolate the outlook to years 2025, 2030 and 2035. In this exercise, the key data points we need to pay attention to are:

a. There will be more than 55,000 Singapore residents celebrating their 65th birthdays every year, for the 40 years from 2021 to 2060 – more and more people drawing down on CPF funds with fewer economically productive young people contributing to CPF?

b. There will be more than 1 million Singapore residents (Singaporeans and Permanent Residents) who are 65 years or older in 2035 – will healthcare facilities and retirement homes be sufficient?

c. Sometime on or before year 2030, the number of deaths will exceed the numbers of births at around 37,000 and thereafter, the death numbers will increase rapidly, to above 50,000 per year in 2035 – will there be sufficient buyers for the flats that will come onto the resale market?

d. The number of HDB flats put on the resale market as a result of the passing of the remaining owner will range from a low-end estimate of 2,400 units per year in 2025 to a high-end estimate of 11,400 units per year in 2035. See Table 1.

Table 1: Estimated number of HDB flats put on the resale market as a result of the passing away of the remaining owner for the three years of 2025, 2030 and 2035.

	Lower-bound estimate	Upper-bound estimate
2025	2,424	4,268
2030	3,395	8,129
2035	4,093	11,401

Source: International Property Advisor

Our range of estimates would improve if we had data for Singapore citizens' death rates instead of residents' death rates. Unfortunately the Department of Statistics would not sell that data to us in 2017 and I did not bother making another request this year. Also, there is a lack of published data on the number of households living in each HDB dwelling unit and whether the units are jointly owned by a couple, by a parent and a child or purely in the surviving spouse's name.

Regardless, the rising number of Silent Generation and Baby Boomers passing away will not reverse unless medical science creates a miracle longevity pill. Investments in healthcare, end-of-life and silver-hair businesses will/should take priority over investments in residential properties.

Even with these data laid out clearly, Singaporeans continue to believe that asset enhancement programmes will perpetually grow their retirement nest eggs.

"Just buy! The government will not let us die." Singaporeans have such high expectations that the government will save us from our own folly!

Cautioned for trying to do a favour?

It is with these concerns in mind that when I was invited by a journalist in 2018 to write opinion pieces for *The Straits Times* about these public housing issues, I immediately took up the challenge. In "Prepare for supply avalanche as ageing HDB flat owners die" published on 5 March 2018, I discussed the impact of the ageing population and deaths contributing to a rise in resale HDB flats. In a second piece published on 14 August 2018 titled "Outdated ideas on home ownership and land shortage are crippling us", I urged HDB buyers to be cautious and HDB "owners" to set more reasonable expectations about the value of their flats. I reasoned that since we do not own the flats, we should not be too materially attached to the decaying value and cling on while suffering more losses. I appealed to the common sense of readers to accept this reality so that those who are senior citizens can plan their retirement finances accordingly. But Singaporeans remain stuck on the idea that the HDB flat is a prized asset whose value can only appreciate, ignoring the downward price pressure from depreciating leases.

I had quietly hoped that my opinion pieces will spur policy makers to address this pressing situation of value decay caused by depreciating leases coupled with rising number of deaths and resale flats.

All the public chatter about the depreciating values of old flats finally resulted in some action from the government. At the National Day Rally 2018 on 19 August 2018, Prime Minister Lee Hsien Loong announced:[1]

a. that all HDB flats will be upgraded twice during their 99 years lease

b. a new Voluntary Early Redevelopment Scheme (VERS) for flats which are more than 70 years old[2]

However, as the upgrading scheme and VERS are still more than a decade or two down the road, there were no details as to the criteria and conditions under which they would be implemented. In fact, while upgrading will allow the physical state of the flats to comfortably house residents for many more years, it is unclear how the asset value will be maintained as the lease runs into its final 40 years. As for VERS, it is also unclear how the authorities will prioritise the redevelopment if, when the time comes and a dozen estates concurrently vote to proceed with VERS. To many observers, these measures seem to have been announced somewhat prematurely. Meanwhile, the lease depreciation and value decline continue, and the problem is deferred further into the future.

And then, five days later, at a book launch event on 24 August 2018, the Prime Minister refuted the notion of HDB flats being long term rentals, saying: "I find this argument frankly amazing. Many private properties are held on 99-year leases too, and yet nobody argues that they are merely being rented."[3]

---

1 https://www.channelnewsasia.com/news/singapore/home-ownership-hdb-helps-singapo-reans-build-assets-pm-lee-10648722

2 Alfred Chua, "All HDB flats to get upgrading twice during 99-year leases", *Today*, 19 August 2018, https://www.todayonline.com/singapore/all-hdb-flats-get-upgrading-twice-during-99-year-leases

3 https://www.straitstimes.com/politics/pm-lee-hsien-loong-rebuts-notion-that-99-year-hdb-lease-is-extended-rental-not-a-sale
https://www.todayonline.com/singapore/singapores-homeownership-and-asset-enhance-ment-policies-have-worked-well-pm-lee

Oddly, several media chose to make reference the opinion piece I contributed to *The Straits Times*. The articles mentioned the same thing: that while the Prime Minister did not name the commentators he referred to as "frankly amazing", a commentary published by *The Straits Times* on 14 August where International Property Advisor chief executive Ku Swee Yong recommended "that we be honest with ourselves and recognise that we are merely lessees who rent the HDB flats for their terms". It was probably a coincidence that the journalists lifted off the exact same quote from my opinion piece and not refer to some press release or coordinated statement.

Other senior government officials chimed in on this subject. Two weeks after the Prime Minister's "frankly amazing" comment, housing Minister Lawrence Wong emphasized at a HDB forum for real estate professionals on 4 September 2018, that the "claims that HDB flat buyers do not own their flats and are renting them is "factually and legally wrong". He said that "there is also no basis to such a claim".

Oops, seems that I have been warned publicly. But this statement confused me and members of the public further.

Over the years, well more than 2 million people must have signed on the Agreement for Lease, Memorandum of Lease and the Lease documents with the Housing & Development Board before they took their keys to their HDB flats. And in these contracts, the position of HDB being a Lessor and landlord relative to the obligations of the flat "owner" or the Lessee (which is also defined as the "Purchaser") seems rather clear. Unless my understanding of the English language has serious short-comings, I am unable to see from these documents which parts might be "factually and legally wrong" to consider the HDB flat "owner" as someone who owns a long-term lease and is in fact a tenant in his flat. The documents also read to me that the HDB "owner" does not have full ownership of the flat as there are binding covenants about what the "owner" can and cannot do with the flat, e.g. to pay an annual rent of $1 on top of the "purchase" price, to pledge it to a business partner for a loan, to not keep pets, to permit entry by the Lessor, etc. etc. In fact, the covenants in the Memorandum of Lease read rather similar to those in tenancy agreements for private residential properties.

Fig. 3: The cover page of a sample of the Agreement for Lease available for reference on HDB's website

THIS AGREEMENT FOR LEASE is made the

Between the Housing and Development Board (hereinafter called "the Board") a body corporate incorporated under the Housing and Development Act (hereinafter called "the Act") and having its office at HDB Hub, 480 Lorong 6 Toa Payoh, Singapore 310480 of the one part and

(hereinafter together called "the Purchaser") of the other part.

WHEREAS:

1   The Board has under Part IV of the Act and in reliance of statements and representations made by the Purchaser agreed to sell and the Purchaser has agreed to purchase the premises more particularly described in the First Schedule hereto (hereinafter called "the Flat") on the terms and conditions hereinafter contained

2   The Purchaser has paid the Board a sum of $_____ being the option fee for the purchase of the Flat (hereinafter called "the option fee").

IT IS HEREBY AGREED as follows:

1   Subject to the provisions contained in Part IV of the Act and as hereinafter contained the Board shall grant and the Purchaser shall accept a Lease of the Flat together with and subject to the various rights easements privileges and reservations more particularly set out and specified in the form of Lease annexed hereto marked "A" (hereinafter called "the Lease") and the Memorandum of Lease annexed hereto marked "B" (hereinafter called "the Memorandum of Lease") all of which annexures are subscribed by the Purchaser for the purpose of identification for a term of 99 years from the _____ day of _____ in consideration of the sum of $_____ (hereinafter called "the Purchase Price") to be paid by the Purchaser in accordance with Clause 3 hereof and yielding and paying therefor during the said term free from all deductions a yearly rent of Dollar One ($1/-) payable without demand the first payment to be made without apportionment on the date when the Purchaser takes possession of the Flat and thereafter on the first day of January of each year.

01.04.2011   1

Source: http://www10.hdb.gov.sg/fi10/fi10297p.nsf/ImageView/Specimen%20AFL/$file/Specimen+AFL.pdf

Fig. 4: The cover page of a sample of the Lease of the physical premises (i.e. the flat) available for reference on HDB's website.

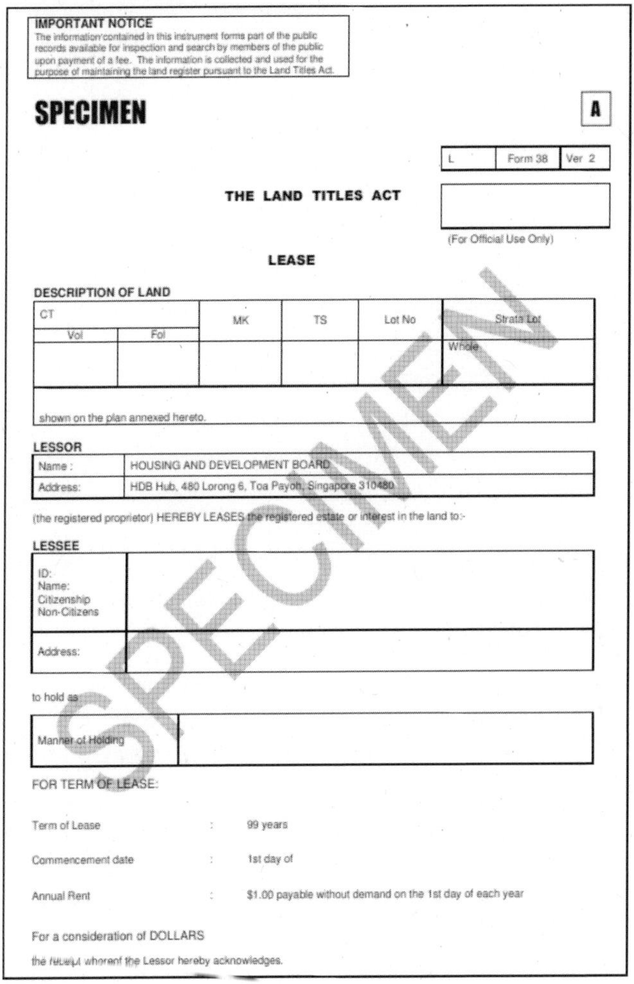

IMPORTANT NOTICE
The information contained in this instrument forms part of the public records available for inspection and search by members of the public upon payment of a fee. The information is collected and used for the purpose of maintaining the land register pursuant to the Land Titles Act.

SPECIMEN

| | Form 3B | Ver 2 |

A

THE LAND TITLES ACT

(For Official Use Only)

LEASE

DESCRIPTION OF LAND

CT		MK	TS	Lot No	Strata Lot
Vol	Fol				Whole

shown on the plan annexed hereto.

LESSOR

Name :	HOUSING AND DEVELOPMENT BOARD
Address:	HDB Hub, 480 Lorong 6, Toa Payoh, Singapore 310480

(the registered proprietor) HEREBY LEASES the registered estate or interest in the land to:-

LESSEE

ID: Name: Citizenship Non-Citizens	
Address:	

to hold as

Manner of Holding	

FOR TERM OF LEASE:

Term of Lease	:	99 years
Commencement date	:	1st day of
Annual Rent	:	$1.00 payable without demand on the 1st day of each year

For a consideration of DOLLARS

the receipt whereof the Lessor hereby acknowledges.

Source: https://www.hdb.gov.sg/cs/infoweb/-/media/doc/EAPG/specimen-lease.pdf

The discussions and debate went on. Even up till 19 March 2019, Minister Heng Swee Keat was quoted at a real estate industry event by *Today*:

> Mr Heng also dismissed criticisms that HDB dwellers are merely tenants instead of owners.
>
> "This debate that is going on… (People saying), 'No, this is a terrible hoax… This is macam (like) rental', I mean, come on, get real," he asserted.[4]

But by late 2018, the fake news law or POFMA (Protection from Online Falsehoods and Manipulation Act) was already tabled for discussion in parliament. I received words of advice and caution from well-wishers, friends, classmates, relatives, naysayers, etc. that I should stop discussing the issue of the decaying HDB leases. On the other hand, several lawyers and academics said that I will not be "POFMA-ed" as long as I am expressing my opinion, especially if the opinions are backed up by research and references.

The act was passed into law on 8 May 2019. I decided to stop speaking to the mainstream media but continued with my research on public housing issues.

Fourth major piece about FOSG proposal

In mid-2019, renowned architect and Adjunct Professor Tay Kheng Soon contacted me. He was working on a comprehensive proposal about Singapore's public housing together with ex-GIC Chief Economist Yeoh Lam Keong. The proposal was facilitated by the Future Of Singapore Group (FOSG), a non-partisan internet research and discussion forum, and it wanted to tackle the challenges of the

---

4 Janice Lim, "HDB flats still have value when owner reaches 85 years old: Heng Swee Keat", *Today*, 19 March 2019, https://www.todayonline.com/singapore/hdb-flats-still-have-value-when-owner-reaches-85-years-old-heng-swee-keat

physical deterioration of old HDB blocks and their lease decay and value depreciation vis-à-vis the seemingly inadequate retirement wealth of the average Singaporean. This joint proposal by Prof Tay, Yeoh Lam Keong and me is the most recent piece of my work on HDB, before this book chapter that is.

The final proposal was presented at a public forum on 30 November 2019 at the Singapore Management University. You can read the suggested solutions in Chapter 17, "Addressing Singapore's Key Public Housing Problems: Asset Protection, Affordability and Access". You may also watch the public forum's presentation and audience Q&A on my YouTube channel "Ku Swee Yong Real Estate": https://www.youtube.com/playlist?list=PLYu5iJQRHcvM5Z msnEgILVu1bpVSveOlY

Our challenges in public housing

Major challenges await us in the next 10 years. By 2030, more than 500,000 flats will have less than 60 years of lease left, i.e. more than 40 years old. From that age, the flat's value falls quickly towards $0 as the pool of buyers shrink due to restrictions on age, loans and CPF usage. The physical deterioration of the flats may be more advanced as well.

By 2030, the pool of resale flats arising from deaths and inheritance will increase to as high as 8,100 units a year, adding significant downward pressure on resale prices. It could exceed 11,000 flats a year in 2035.

We need to address these issues really soon and one way to start is to lower expectations about the "nest egg" that HDB flats are, or are not.

One writer to *The Straits Times* Forum pages summed it up nicely:

> "Calling HDB buyers homeowners works to perpetuate the misconception that they own the flat outright. This results in serious and damaging misunderstandings.
>
> … This is made worse when we refer to HDB flats as "nest eggs" which will continue to appreciate."
>
> Cheah Wenjie, 21 July 2017[5]

However, the road ahead is an uphill one. I often see advertisements on various social media and websites of mainstream media placed by the Government of Singapore titled "Do I Really Own My HDB Flat". I find these write-ups confusing as the concept of 99-year HDB lease, 99-year leasehold title and rental agreements are too briefly, and thus not clearly, explained. The layman will probably be even more confused.

Fig. 5: An example of an advertisement on the internet that links to the answers provided by the government which links to https://www.gov.sg/article/do-i-really-own-my-hdb-flat

Do I Really Own My HDB Flat

Read More

Government of Singapore

---

5 Cheah Wenjie, "HDB was describing a lease ownership", *The Straits Times* Forum, 21 July 2017, https://www.straitstimes.com/forum/letters-in-print/hdb-was-describing-a-lease-ownership

While the old flats continue to depreciate in value, more and more million-dollar flats in prime locations are being transacted. In 10 to 20 years' time, today's million-dollar flats similarly become old flats and depreciate. This time, the value will drop from a much higher price level. A December 2020 article backed by lots of transacted data was written by Kyle Leung from 99.co. He cautioned that the exuberance and hype around million-dollar HDB flats could be masking a longer-term, more worrisome trend of old flats, in the same towns as the million-dollar flats, trading at lower and lower prices. The uptrend of the HDB resale index in 2020 does not tell the full story.[6]

As for new HDB flats, with weaker economic growth expected in future, a trending gig-economy, weaker employment prospects and slower income growth for most of the younger families, we need to get serious about making HDB flats affordable for more families. The new Minister for National Development, Mr Desmond Lee, assumed his position after the July 2020 general elections. He has since changed the HDB CEO and gave us a first glimpse into his concerns about public housing.

In a Facebook post on 11 December 2020, the new minister said that as new flats get built in prime locations near the CBD, such as in the future Greater Southern Waterfront, the prices of these new flats will be more expensive and therefore, higher grants would be needed for young families so to maintain affordability. With the higher grants, there will likely be more restrictions on the resale of these flats, such that the "lottery effect" for sellers will be capped and resale buyers will continue to find prices affordable.[7]

---

6 Kyle Leung, "Million-dollar HDB flats are hiding a worrying resale price trend. Here's proof.", 99.co, December 2020, https://www.99.co/blog/singapore/million-dollar-hdb-flats-are-hiding a worrying-resale-price-trend-heres-proof/
7 Michelle Ng, "BTO flats in prime locations may get more govt subsidies but face resale restrictions: Desmond Lee", The Straits Times, 11 December 2020, https://www.straits-times.com/singapore/housing/new-housing-model-necessary-for-new-bto-flats-in-prime-locations-desmond-lee

Perhaps the issue of new HDB flats in prime locations, such as Pinnacle at Duxton, might open up another vigorous debate amongst the public about fairness, entitlement and windfalls at the expense of tax payers' grants and public housing subsidies.

The minister and the new CEO of HDB have just started in their roles. Many current public housing "owners" are awaiting to see how they will take on the challenges posed by the ageing population and the value decay of old flats.

I hope it will be soon.

Note: I am thankful for the research on the forward estimates of resident deaths and additional resale HDB flats undertaken by undergraduates from Singapore Management University: Benjamin Tan Ting Cher, Chan Min Rachel, Esther Ng Li Ting, Justin Wong Yi Jie, Sophia Chow Hui Ru and Wang Sijie.

7. Can this 'CPF Key' Truly Unlock the Value for Old Flats?

Co-authored with Joel Kam; first published on PropertySoul.com, 11 August 2019

In May 2019, the government relaxed rules for older people looking to buy old flats using more money from their CPF accounts. The aim of amending the rules was primarily to improve the demand for older flats, so that the value of older flats may be maintained for longer.[1]

One of the examples quoted in the Ministry of Manpower's press release described a couple, John (age 48) and Jane (age 45), who are buying an old 4-room flat with 50 years left on the lease. The age of Jane, the youngest buyer, and the remaining lease equals to 95 years in total, satisfying the new criteria for using CPF to fund their purchase in full. The price of the flat is $430,000. Under the new rules, all $430,000 may be paid from the couple's CPF accounts. Under the previous rules, CPF usage was capped at 80% of the value of the old flat, i.e. $344,000. Thus, the new rules allow the buyers an increase of $86,000 CPF usage.

---

1 "More Flexibility to Buy a Home for Life While Safeguarding Retirement Adequacy", Ministry of Manpower, 9 May 2019, https://www.mom.gov.sg/newsroom/press-releases/2019/0509-more-flexibility to buy a home-for-life

Market watchers were quick to highlight the benefits of the change of rules, pointing out that the new rules will "help unlock values of older houses that were artificially depressed by the previous CPF rules."[2]

The values of older flats will be unlocked. Really? What gives?

(Note: For the purpose of our discussion, we define 'old' or 'older' flats to be over 40 years age, which means that these flats have less than 59 years of lease remaining. That is when financing restrictions begin, such that the number of buyers taper down, adding downward pressure on the resale value.)

Let us review if John and Jane's purchase of the 49-year-old 4-room flat with $430,000 of CPF fund was a prudent one.

What if things don't go as planned?

Firstly, did John and Jane consider that their plans could go awry and exigencies might pop up during their retirement years? What if they desperately needed to sell their flat 15 years down the road, will there be many families willing, and able, to buy the remaining lease of 35 years on this flat?

a. Potential buyers who would like to make full use of their CPF would have to be 60 years old and above.

b. Buyers below 60 years age would need to supplement their purchase with cash.

c. Any buyers above 55 years of age would likely have cashed out their CPF down to the Full Retirement Sum (FRS) or for those who are richer, the Enhanced Retirement Sum (ERS). They would only be able to use money in excess of the Basic Retirement Sum (BRS).

---

2 Kuan Wen-Mei Eileen and Sing Tien Foo, "A CPF key to unlocking values of older homes", *Today*, 14 June 2019, https://www.todayonline.com/commentary/cpf-key-unlocking-values-older-homes

THE FUTURE OF REAL ESTATE

d. Based on current CPF rules, pledging a property allows a buyer of age 55 and above to draw down on the CPF retirement account to pay for the house, down to the minimum sum or BRS of $88,000. Drawing down CPF from the FRS to BRS level means $88,000 may be used to purchase the flat. Drawing down from the ERS to the BRS level means $176,000 may be used to purchase the flat. But these come at the expense of the monthly retirement income the buyer can receive from age 65 onwards.

e. For a 60-year-old couple who wish to pay in full with CPF monies, assuming both have maximum ERS, they can afford to pay $176,000 x 2 = $352,000. At this selling price, John and Jane will incur a loss in value of $430,000 – $352,000 = $78,000. A $78,000 depreciation in 15 years (or $5,200 a year), not bad if the old flat is seen as a consumption. But for the 60-year old couple buying at $352,000 for 35 years of use, they lose about $10,000 of their CPF monies per year.

f. How many old couples are able to fork out such a large sum from their CPF, and sacrifice their monthly income after they cross 65 years of age?

g. How many younger couples are willing to purchase the flat? Prospective buyers below 60 years old would only be able to use a pro-rated amount of CPF depending on their age. These buyers would be cognizant that they might outlive the remaining 35 years of the flat's lease.

h. Therefore, John and Jane will have to find buyers who are willing to fund their purchase with cash and CPF.

Which begs the question: how much would buyers be willing to pay John and Jane for a flat with 35 years left on the lease which will certainly depreciate to zero value? Even if VERS (Voluntary Early Redevelopment Scheme) were to take place, what is the compensation that the buyers will receive? Will the compensation also cover relocation costs? What if the vote for VERS did not go through?

Have John and Jane considered carefully?

Secondly, we wish that John and Jane consider carefully whether they should apply $430,000 of their CPF monies to live in this flat for the next 50 years.

a. In the immediate next 20 years of their lives, as John (68) and Jane (65) retire from full-time work and lose their income stream, they have also lost 20 years of interest payment from 2.5% per annum of interest from CPF Ordinary Account (OA) and 4.0% per annum of interest from CPF Retirement Account (RA). Depending on their income and how much was in their CPF OA when they turned 55, John and Jane would lose at least $274,000 of interest income in the next 20 years.

b. By then, the flat's lease would be left with 30 years and a residual value that may be well below half of the $430,000 purchase price. Unless they have a lot of cash for their retirement years, the depreciation of the flat over the next 20 years added to the loss of CPF interest of at least $274,000 would significantly impact their retirement. They have little option to monetise their flat's value except leasing out spare bedrooms.

c. If John and Jane were to live to the ripe old ages of 98 and 95, their HDB flat would have zero value and they would be without a roof over their heads at a time when they are most in need.

d. At their current age of 48 and 45, while they are still healthy and earning a steady income, they should consider using less CPF funds and taking a 15-year loan to afford a younger flat even if it is more expensive.

What's our conclusion?

Early data collected from the first two months after the relaxation of the rules seem to indicate that the transactions of old HDB flats have increased. However, the authors of the research might have overlooked that the stock of old flats has increased substantially over the past year.[3]

---

3 Fiona Lam, "CPF, loan rule changes reinvigorate demand for older HDB flats: OrangeTee", *The Business Times*, 6 August 2019, https://www.businesstimes.com.sg/real-estate/cpf-loan-rule-changes-reinvigorate-demand-for-older-hdb-flats-orangetee

While there may be a greater number of middle-aged buyers below 55 who will be eligible to buy old flats fully funded by CPF, the increase in the age-sum from 80 to 95 years also means fewer younger people are able to pay in full for the old flats using CPF, which means demand from younger buyers will be reduced.

We also doubt that the relaxation of the rules would appeal to people who are above the age of 55 and have their savings inside their retirement account (RA). Leaving their CPF inside their RA earns them a minimum of 4% per annum, a steep interest to give up in exchange for buying a property which will continuously depreciate.

Therefore, it is tough to argue for the case that the overall demand for old flats will increase and that the prices of old flats will be uplifted.

We urge older buyers to carefully consider their full options, including long-term renting, to reduce the risks of being unable to monetize their flats and have their hands tied during retirement years.

8. Addressing Singapore's Key Public Housing Problems: Asset Protection, Affordability and Access

Authored by Tay Kheng Soon, Yeoh Lam Keong and Ku Swee Yong

A citizen's nonpartisan policy proposal, this paper was first published on the *Future of Singapore* website on 30 November 2019, presented before the public and subsequently submitted to the Ministry of National Development. It is reproduced here with minor edits and formatting changes.

EXECUTIVE SUMMARY
Background and introduction

Singapore has a stellar reputation in having achieved the most extensive, high quality and successful national housing programme in the OECD. The proposals in this paper seek to address the key long-term crises in HDB-managed housing and to improve upon it. There are two major problems facing HDB housing today:

First, HDB flat owners have no long-term security of tenure nor any assurance that the capital values of their flats will be preserved at the end of the 99-year lease. As a result, their life savings will depreciate significantly as they age.

As things currently stand, the value of HDB flats will become zero at the end of their 99-year lease, unless they are fortunate enough to qualify for Selective En bloc Redevelopment Scheme (SERS) midway. However, for the bottom 50% of income earners, the bulk of their net worth or life savings is in the value of their HDB flat. For most of them, when their flats go beyond the 40-50 year old mark, the value of HDB flats tends to decline rapidly, just when the owners need to capitalize on their flats' values to fund their retirement the most. Neither the proposed Voluntary Early Redevelopment Scheme (VERS), the Short-lease Flexi flats nor the Lease Buyback Scheme (LBS) currently adequately addresses this problem.

Secondly, the current cost of HDB flats for first-time buyers of BTO flats relative to their incomes is very high, with the result that it typically takes about 25 years for home buyers to pay off their housing loans. This effectively means that for the greater part of their working lives, many Singaporeans are channelling a significant part of their disposable incomes to paying off their HDB flats, leaving insufficient savings for retirement, medical expenses and education upgrading. The problem is exacerbated for the lower, irregular or uncertain incomes that makes home ownership difficult.

The challenge is to craft reform proposals which not only address the concerns identified above, but which are also affordable, fiscally responsible and do not destabilize the existing housing market. To this end, this paper proposes **four major reforms** to HDB managed housing that will address these problems and greatly improve the well-being of all Singapore citizens.

1. Extension of lease

In order to preserve the value of older HDB flats, our first proposal is that the Government should do a one-time automatic top up of the leases of all HDB flats owned by Singapore citizens back to 99 years once a HDB flat is 50 years old. This immediately addresses the problem of declining residual values of old HDB flats with short remaining leases. The lease top-up cost should be priced affordably at around 3% of the price of a new resale flat, with support for low-income families to enable all citizens to afford it, much like current HDB upgrading schemes.

2. Replacement of aged flats

The first proposal above brings with it a technical issue which needs to be solved: All reinforced concrete flats need to be torn down and rebuilt on a 100-150 year horizon for structural safety reasons. Accordingly, our second proposal is that the Government fund the rebuilding cost of all HDB flats every 100 years. The total bill for such a nation-wide exercise is estimated at $150-200 billion dollars over 100 years. While the cost of this programme is large over the long term, it is nevertheless eminently affordable and sustainable when amortized over 100 years.

It is proposed that the Government fund this exercise by setting aside $1.5-2 billion annually (a mere 0.3-0.4% of current GDP) into a sinking fund for this purpose. As with the current SERS, a fresh 99-year lease should be given to all HDB flat owning citizens after rebuilding.

3. New pricing policy of new flats

The third proposal is that all new BTO flats be sold at around construction cost of $150-200 psf. Such flats will not be eligible for sale in the resale market for the first 15 years to help effectively safeguard the price of current resale flats. One family can only own one such flat at a time. Flat owners older than age 65 should also be allowed the option to downgrade once to a smaller, low-cost BTO flat to further boost retirement adequacy.

4. Social rental housing

The fourth proposal is that for citizens who still cannot afford home ownership, sufficient numbers of good quality, subsidized rental flats be maintained with a reasonable security of lease tenure. This is needed to ensure that housing is affordable to all, especially for the less well-off in the gig economy with increasingly unstable employment.

Fiscal implications

These reforms are eminently affordable and fiscally sustainable, and will leave substantial fiscal resources available for other important major budget items. The proposals will preserve the life savings of the population invested in HDB flats, especially the bottom 50% of income earners, thus reducing the need for what would otherwise be larger state retirement income support.

Long-term positive macroeconomic impact

At the macro level, these reforms will greatly help overall retirement adequacy, especially for our elderly poor (Section 3). It will boost domestic demand through lower "forced savings" and therefore greater consumption. There is also the fiscal boost of continuous rebuilding of the housing stock which will be renewed to best architectural standards every 100 years. Additionally, these proposals will also ensure all new flat buyers will be able to afford high quality flats that they can fully pay off in 10-15 years. This will release more savings for retirement and entrepreneurial activity which are currently locked up in housing while minimizing the negative impact on the values of resale flats. The proposed reforms are not expected to destabilize either the existing HDB resale market nor the private housing market.

Social well-being and intergenerational benefits

At the level of social well-being, these reforms will not only ensure Singapore citizens the very significant security of being able to both afford and live in the flat they purchase until the end of life but will also enable them to preserve their flat's value as either an asset to monetize in retirement or a bequest to the next generation. This further helps sustain the social networks needed for happy ageing in-situ as well as for long-term community building. The rental reforms will also address the basic housing needs of the less well-off in the uncertain labour markets of the future.

Towards a Renewed Social Compact
The value proposition to these four major proposed HDB reforms, amounting to a new social compact, is that any citizen will be able to reasonably afford a flat that will preserve its value and be rebuilt to a high and safe standard across successive generations. All citizens will have access to affordable, high quality housing that suits them, be it ownership or rental. This will be a level of public housing achievement tied to citizens' rights that will be unparalleled anywhere in the world. It will give Singapore citizenship a substantial new value and meaning.

In the face of growing retirement inadequacy with a rapidly ageing population, increasing employment uncertainty as well as inherently expensive housing costs due to our limited land size, it is important for Singaporeans to capitalise on our fiscal, public land ownership and organisational strengths to reform current HDB policy to attain the full potential of public housing for the good of all citizens.

The Structure of this Proposal
Section 1 outlines the key problems facing public housing in HDB today and focuses on the dynamics of declining lease values over time and the severe adverse implications for life savings, especially for the bottom 50% of income earners.

Section 2 discusses problems of affordability of HDB flats for first-time buyers and the poor as well as the likely growing numbers of citizens with uncertain incomes in the volatile and fragmented labour markets of the future.

Section 3 proposes a solution to the problem of sharply declining HDB flat values past year 50 of a flat's lease tenure in the form of an affordable lease extension process and suggests some approaches to the rationale of pricing such lease extensions. Ultimately, we propose simple guidelines to a subsidised system of such pricing to ensure universal affordability based on the premise that HDB leases are a unique public good in the first instance, and should not be taken as a market-driven asset. It also discusses the technical need for rebuilding HDB estates every 100 years to ensure structural integrity and usability and proposes that the Government pay for this eventual rebuilding from an eminently affordable annual 'sinking fund'.

Section 4 discusses the benefits and the broad positive macroeconomic impact of such measures on retirement adequacy, household savings, technological advancements and economic growth.

Section 5 argues the case for the fiscal sustainability of such measures while not crowding out other needed major budgetary spending.

Section 6 discusses the proposed solutions to the thorny dilemma of the need for affordable new BTO flats while at the same time maintaining the value of existing resale flats. It proposes all new BTOs be sold at around construction cost as well as the need for an adequate supply of good quality, HDB rental flats. It makes an important suggestion that such low-priced BTO flats be segmented from the resale market for the first 10-15 years to preserve the current value of resale HDB flats. It also argues that HDB flat owners at age 65 should be entitled to downgrade to a smaller low-cost BTO flat to help fund their retirement adequacy owing to rapid demographic ageing and growing longevity.

Section 7 concludes.

Section 1: Pressing Issues for HDB Reform

There are two major problems needing important reforms in HDB-managed public housing.

Firstly, there is a long-term crisis facing all HDB flat owners, particularly lower income Singaporeans. HDB flat owners have no long-term security of tenure nor any assurance that the capital values of their flats will be preserved at the end of the 99-year lease. This adversely affects their life savings, a significant part of which has been invested in their flats and which will depreciate significantly. This problem will accelerate over time, particularly as the current stock of flats grow older.

Secondly, the current cost of HDB flats for first-time buyers of BTO flats relative to their incomes is very high, with the result that it typically takes about 25-30 years for home buyers to pay off their housing loans. This effectively means that for the greater part of their working lives, many Singaporeans are channelling a significant part of their disposable incomes to paying off their HDB flats, leaving insufficient savings for retirement, medical expenses and education upgrading. This is in contrast to the first 20 years of HDB's history when loans could be paid off in 10-15 years. The problem is exacerbated for the lower income and those with irregular or uncertain incomes who may not even be able to afford homes.

The challenge is to craft reform proposals which not only properly address the concerns identified above but which are also affordable, fiscally responsible and do not destabilize the existing residential property market. There is good reason for confidence that the proposals articulated in this paper achieve all of these objectives.

We discuss each problem separately below.

Current HDB flats are "sold" on a 99-year lease. There is no assurance nor is there any obligation on the part of the Government to renew these leases upon the end of their tenure. In any event, the conditions for lease renewal post 99-years have, thus far, not been articulated by the Government.

Hence, as things presently stand, absent SERS which offers HDB owners an attractive, often above market compensation and a resettlement grant to buy a new HDB flat, the lease reverts to the HDB at the end of 99 years and the residual value of the HDB flat falls to zero.

SERS does not adequately address the first problem identified. It is currently applied to less than 5% of HDB flats, leaving 95% of HDB owners still facing the problem of zero capital value at the end of their 99-year leases.

A new scheme called VERS (voluntary early redevelopment scheme) announced in August 2018 suggested that flats which are 70 years and older to be sold back to HDB en bloc at *prevailing market prices*, with the sales proceeds utilized to purchase a new HDB flat *at that point in time, and provided a undetermined majority voted for it.* Details of the scheme are still pending but, at first glance, compensation under VERS does not look as attractive as compared to SERS because the flats will be much older and, thus have a much smaller residual value. Market analysts expect the residual values of these ageing flats to be closer to the much lower resale prices of such older flats.[1] This is confirmed by the analysis below.

The underlying value of older flats with remaining lease tenures of 50 years or less tends to follow the table used by SLA and HDB for

---

1 For details on LBS, SERS and VERS please see: https://www.hdb.gov.sg/cs/infoweb/
residential/living-in-an-hdb-flat/for-our-seniors/leasebuyback-scheme, https://blog.
moneysmart.sg/property/sers-vers-hdb-en-bloc-sale-schemes/ and https://www.todayon-
line.com/commentary/why-hdb-owners-should-forget-aboutgetting-windfall-vers

valuing leaseholds called "Bala's Table", shown in the graph below. It is used as a guideline under the Lease Buyback Scheme (LBS) currently available to HDB owners (see Fig 1 below). Bala's Table shows that as HDB flats age and approach 70-80 years old, their values are likely to drop significantly to about 40-50% of the value of equivalent new flats. The table further shows that under current terms, the flat has no residual value at the end of the 99-year lease.

Fig. 1: Underlying Trends in HDB Leasehold Values Over Time (Bala's Table)

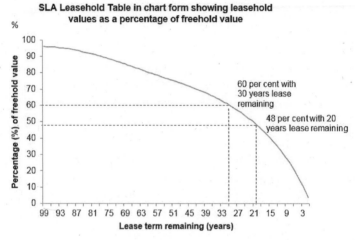

Source: Christopher Gee, *https://www.todayonline.com/commentary/why-hdb-owners-should-forget-about-getting-windfall-vers*

Furthermore, Bala's Table also represents the most optimistic resale value of these flats without taking into account financing and physical constraints. It does not, for example, take into account the deterioration, usability, maintenance and financing restrictions of such old flats. There is, therefore, good reason to believe that the market values of these much older flats will in fact be lower than those suggested by Bala's Table.

To illustrate this point, bank loans are not available for purchasing flats with 30 or less years remaining, HDB loans are not available

| THE FUTURE OF REAL ESTATE

to purchase flats with 20 or less years remaining on the lease. Middle-aged buyers of old flats who are concerned about retirement adequacy may want to leave more CPF monies to accumulate and therefore set a lower budget for the purchase of old flats knowing that the old flats will depreciate towards zero value. This has a clear negative implication for the values of ageing HDB flats. Flats with less than 60 years of remaining lease have limited resale value as the CPF and loan for the unit's subsequent buyer would be more restricted. In anticipation of such disadvantageous financing conditions and the consequently shrinking pool of resale buyers, markets are likely to accelerate the natural price decline even further after a flat reaches 40-50 years of age.

VERS and the LBS, which at least guarantee the Government as purchaser of old flats, is of limited utility in preventing this substantial depreciation and the resultant loss of savings, since Government compensation values for such short leases are based on the then prevailing resale market prices for such aged flats, possibly with a further discount for the time value of money. The cumulative effect is that asset values of HDB flats will correspondingly have fallen by 30-40%, or even more, due to resale and other limitations by the time a flat reaches 70 years of age when it becomes eligible for VERS. Furthermore, VERS is envisaged to be voluntary and is subject to whether there is a majority of the owners who will vote for the programme.

The LBS, in turn, enables some older HDB owners to sell the last 35 years of their leases to top up their CPF LIFE retirement plans and possibly obtain a cash pay out with a small cash bonus. However, as Bala's and similar tables show, the value of 40-50 year old HDB flats could have already fallen 15-20% when they are typically being considered for LBS and is likely to fall even more steeply after that. HDB flat owners' net asset value available for retirement would have therefore diminished significantly right at the time when they need to capitalize or liquidate the value of their remaining leases to fund their medical and retirement needs! LBS is also unpopular as it is designed to leave no bequest value after the owners pass away, something important to Asian families.

This prospect of rapidly declining values of HDB flats after 40-50 years, coupled with the uncertainty of lease renewal terms and conditions (if any), is causing the market value of older HDB flats to fall rapidly. HDB owners thus face the prospect of rapidly declining life savings, particularly as they and their flats advance in age.

The price fall most heavily impacts the life savings of the bottom 50% of citizens as 75-90% of their net worth is tied up in the value of their HDB flats.[2]

There is, therefore, both a significant price decline and consequently a savings crisis developing in the 50-year and older HDB leasehold market in Singapore. Chart 2 below is taken from the average transaction prices of 3-room flats around 50 years old in Blk 9 Lor 7 Toa Payoh compiled by property agent, Mr Timothy Quek.

From the transacted prices in Chart 2, one can see that after the hard truth of the net residual value of HDB flats was discussed in March 2017, the value of old HDB flats in Toa Payoh fell sharply. This shows quite clearly, albeit from a small sample, the potential for rapid significant decline in the price of old flats once buyers realise that, on current terms, these flats have zero value at the end of their 99 years lease.

---

2 While detailed breakdowns of net worth by asset for different income percentiles are unavailable to the public, the fact that HDB flat values form 75-90% of the net worth of the bottom 50% of the population can be inferred from available data. A 2016 Credit Suisse report shows Singaporeans' average net worth is around $345,000. The average price of a resale 3-room HDB flat is around $350,000 and a 4-room flat around $469,000 in the 2016-2018 period. Please see: https://www.todayonline.com/business/singaporeans-average-wealth-increasesus277000-credit-suisse-report. It can therefore reasonably be inferred that for the bottom 50% of the population, the value of their HDB flat forms the bulk of their net worth.

Mr Quek further stated that in his opinion, in the coming years, "Those buyers above who paid more than $280,000 for these flats today will make a terrible loss." Mr Quek added, "If you intend to sell your HDB flat, you should consider selling it soon before its lease declines further. The prices of HDB flats usually face a sharp decline when they are more than 40 years old when restrictions of using CPF and bank loan to finance their purchase kick in, thereby severely limiting the pool of ready buyers." (Please see https://www. theonlinecitizen.com/2018/11/03/property-agent-very-difficult-to-find-buyers-for-aging-hdb-flats-now/)

Fig. 2: Transaction prices of HDB 3-room flats at Blk 9 Lor 7 Toa Payoh

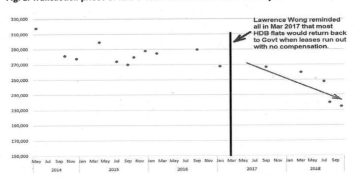

* Figure for Apr 2015 was the average value of 3 transactions in that month

Mr Quek also observed that only 4% of HDB flats have been redeveloped through SERS since 1995. That is, these old flats, typically at very good locations, were repurchased by HDB and the flat owners compensated and relocated. HDB then rebuilt new HDB flats in the same area for subsequent sale to the public.

But the vast majority of flats, Mr Quek noted, will be returned to HDB when their 99-year leases run out, without any compensation. "As the leases run down, especially towards the tail-end, the flat prices will come down correspondingly," he said. "So, buyers need to do their due diligence and be realistic when buying flats with short leases."

This is a real practical problem. There are currently more than 200,000 HDB flats which are more than 40 years old, all facing lease expiry in just over 50 years. The pipeline of such older flats will grow rapidly over the next decade. By the end of 2020, there will be more than 550,000 flats which are more than 30 years old (out of which more than 220,000 are over 40 years age) and which will face the same predicament over the subsequent 10-20 years. This forms nearly half of the total stock of 1,062,350 HDB flats that house around 80% of our resident population. (Please see https://likedatosocanmeh.wordpress.com/2017/04/19/350000-or-480387-hdb-flatsolder-than-30-years/).

Fig. 3: Number of HBD dwelling units constructed

- Includes DBSS Flats of 616 units for 2006 - 2010, and 8,034 units for 2011 - 2015.
- Total number of flats demolished: 126,738
Source: HDB, IPA

Again, the core challenge here is that the value of HDB flats form 75-90% of the net worth of the bottom half of Singapore citizens. If the value decline of these old HDB flats is not addressed, the bulk of the life savings of 50% of Singaporeans will fall significantly as they age, exacerbating retirement adequacy and financial anxiety.

There is the also the possible adverse perception of the Government having failed to live up to its promise of HDB flats being a reliable store of long term value to meet retirement needs and wealth transfer to the next generation. (Please see: https://www.theonlinecitizen. com/2019/03/20/heng-swee-keats-story-about-old-hdb-flatsshows-he-is-grasping-at-straws/).

Section 2: The Problem of Affordability of HDB Flats

We discuss affordability of new BTO flats by reference to prices of new flats in a major integrated new town like Punggol or, more recently, Tengah. Currently, an outer-lying 3-room BTO flat (say in Punggol) costs around $215,000 while a 4-room flat costs around $325,000 (before grants). Couples buying such flats typically take the maximum loan tenure of 25 years to pay off these loans utilizing their CPF funds. Buyers using CPF funds to pay mortgages are paying interest expenses while forgoing CPF interest earnings that would contribute to their retirement. This means that for the greater part of their working lives, many Singaporeans are channelling the bulk of their savings to pay off their HDB flats, leaving insufficient savings for big ticket life-cycle financial items like retirement cashflow, education or emergency medical expenditures. (Please refer to https://www.srx.com.sg/hdb/bto)

To lower mortgage repayment to a more reasonable and affordable 10-15 year horizon, the price of HDB flats need to be lowered to around $135,000 for a 3-room flat of 750 sqft and $180,000 for a 4-room flat of 1,000 sqft. This is based on the higher end of estimates of construction costs of $180 psf by leading property and quantity surveying firms such as Arcadis NV. These costs are not expected to rise by more than average wage or inflation rates due to improvements in technology (largely prefab and materials technology) as well as more cost effective design (more medium to low-rise vs high-rise buildings that can house the same numbers more convivially on similar land areas).

This lower, more affordable proposed BTO price is about 55-60% below current resale flat prices of around $350,000 for a 3-room and $470,000 for a 4-room flat in similar areas like Punggol. (Please see https://sg.finance.yahoo.com/news/could-tengah-reallynext-punggol-033800551.html)

An important policy question is whether such low proposed BTO prices will pull down current resale HDB prices, thereby adversely impacting the net worth of existing HDB owners. We believe this can be addressed. To preserve the values of existing HDB flats, we propose that the new low-cost BTO flats can only be resold to the HDB at cost for the first 15 years. We address this issue of preventing these policy reforms from destabilising HDB resale and private housing markets more comprehensively in Section 7 and in Annex 2.

Low income families, particularly those in the bottom-three deciles, may still be unable to afford the monthly mortgage payments of these lower priced BTO flats, even over 15 years. Owing to the HDB's current policy bias for home ownership, there is an insufficient supply of decent-sized, subsidised rental flats for poor families, which are also often badly overcrowded.[3] (Reference: Singstat Household Income Trends 2019 Table 14A $1583 per household member per month including full CPF and transfers.)

These problems will be exacerbated by current global trends. The evidence indicates that in the longer term, there is an increasing likelihood that there will be a structural shift away from permanent jobs to a series of uncertain payments via contract work or what is popularly referred to as the "gig economy". The realistic alternative for a growing number of low and inconsistent income-earning citizens might therefore be to increase the supply of decent, affordable rental public housing rather than encouraging ownership with long

---

[3] On the issue of crowdedness, in rental housing, please see: https://www.ricemedia.co/current-affairs-features-jalan-kukoh-overcrowding-singaporerental-housing/

term mortgage commitments (and failure to earn CPF interest) that these citizens realistically are unlikely to be able to meet.

Section 3: Proposed Solutions to Security of Tenure and Depreciation of Life Savings Invested in HDB

In order to preserve the value of older HDB flats, our first proposal is that the Government should allow a one-time automatic top-up of the leases of all HDB flats owned by Singapore citizens back to 99 years once a HDB flat is 50 years old. This immediately addresses the problem of declining residual values of old HDB flats with short remaining leases.

The Singapore Land Authority (SLA) however, should retain land ownership and reserve the right to redevelop the flats at any time via the HDB should they wish to do so. However, in such cases, affected owners must be given a compensating flat of equivalent use value and location just like under the current SERS. The condition of quality equivalency is to safeguard the quality of housing provided to HDB owners so that living comfort is not compromised.

An affordable fee should be charged for the lease top-up. In this regard, we suggest that the base guideline fee for lease renewal be set at around 3% of the average market value of a new resale HDB flat for those who are able afford it (for a detailed discussion of the rationale, see Annex 1). This works out to around $15,000 for an average 4-room flat priced at $470,000 and $10,000 for an average 3-room flat priced at $350,000. This lease renewal fee can be made payable over 10-15 years with no interest, and thus made universally affordable like HDB upgrading.

However, smaller, nominal affordable fees as low as 10% of this guideline price can be charged for the lease renewal on a means-tested basis to make it affordable for low income owners and retirees. Only citizens qualify for this subsidised lease renewal.

The first proposal above brings with it a technical issue which needs to be solved. All HDB blocks need to be torn down and rebuilt around every 100-150 years. Prof Tay Kheng Soon's research shows that reinforced concrete structures become structurally unsound over this longer time period.[4]

Thus, to enable HDB owners to have ownership rights beyond 99 years without incurring punitive rebuilding costs, our related second proposal is that the cost of tearing down and rebuilding these flats, once they reach 100 years, should be borne by the Government.

We accordingly propose that every HDB flat purchased by a citizen be guaranteed under a scheme in which the cost of rebuilding is borne by the State and a new flat with equivalent environmentally sustainable quality and comfort be returned to the owner every 100 years of the HDB flats' life. A fresh lease of 99 years should also be given to the existing owner upon completion of this necessary rebuilding, thereby ensuring continuity of housing provision as a social good.

This would be the equivalent of having all HDB flats effectively being guaranteed a SERS programme near the end of their 99-year lease. Only Singapore citizens would be eligible for this effectively free rebuilding of old flats. We suggest that citizens bear the cost of housing during the rebuilding period, given the government will bear the cost of rebuilding. PRs would not be eligible and would have to fund the full reconstruction cost of the new flats unless they surrender the remaining lease of the flat to the HDB under existing lease buyback or under compulsory acquisition guidelines.

With these proposed policies on affordable 99-year lease top-ups and effectively free rebuilding, all older HDB flats are likely

---

4 Refer to Dr Rajesh Kumar "Designing Reinforced Concrete for Long Life Span" and Guy Kuelemans (UNSW) "The Problem with Reinforced Concrete"

to maintain value or see a rise in value depending on whether regular maintenance and upgrading managed to prevent excessive physical deterioration. Both the value and security of tenure of all HDB leases will thus be largely protected from ageing, i.e. HDB flats become a real store of value for retirement or bequest to successive generations. New entrants into the public housing system, and resale for downgrading during retirement or for asset division on death ensure HDB property ownership does not ossify and has sufficient turnover to enable social mobility.

Equally important, the net worth and life savings of the bottom 50% of income earners (whose 3- and 4-room flats form the bulk of their net worth) will be protected for the lifetime of the owners even before rebuilding, thus contributing significantly to their pension adequacy.

For those presently with old flats, their prices could also rise sustainably from their present values, resulting in a corresponding one-off significant restoration of wealth to such owners of HDB flats whose values have suffered time decay for the reasons discussed in Section 1. Readers may refer to Annex 3: Two Common HDB Human Stories.

Section 4: Positive Macroeconomic Impact of the Proposals

This progressive wealth boost and continual rebuilding will also have significant positive macroeconomic effects. Firstly, it will substantially enhance retirement adequacy, particularly for the bottom 50% of the population who need it the most. The significantly higher values of old flats will result in higher cash income or pay outs through sales and downgrading or reverse mortgage schemes as the owners age.

Secondly, achieving a higher and more secure net financial worth across 80% of the citizen population with a more bankable HDB asset should result in greater consumption and investment by the general population. The constant rebuilding of the entire HDB stock over 100 years or less will also represent a constant significant fiscal expansion. Taken together, these should boost greater domestic demand, sustainable construction investment related activity and more buoyant GDP growth.

As effective owner of the underlying HDB land, valuations on governments books and hence national reserves will keep increasing when such rebuilding takes place with a small increase in plot ratios. Land values can also be enhanced by building large multifunction podiums beneath flats to increase land efficiency and provide nearby jobs. Hence as with land-related projects like reclamation or SERS, part of the rebuilding cost can be designed as and considered "enhancement of state reserves". [https://www.todayonline.com/singapore/explainer-how-singapore-will-fund-its-s100-billion-effort-mitigate-climate-change-effects]

However, it will still be incumbent on the Government and HDB to do periodic upgrading of older flats to put in new infrastructure such as wiring, plumbing, structural support and new rooms and lifts, as is currently done. As master planner, HDB would still retain the right and ability, as and when it chooses, to reconfigure public housing estates for the greater societal good, provided it gives affected residents a SERS programme as it does now for the small minority of flats. Nothing in our proposal is intended to impair this flexibility or responsibility.

Finally, the renewal of HDB towns every 100 years also presents a huge economic benefit. In the global quest to improve liveability and to attract talent, we need to maintain a leading position as a state-of-the-art smart city. Traditional methods of town planning with distinct zones for residential, commercial, educational and industrial activities are giving way to multi-purpose buildings and mixed developments within the same zone. The future is a mix of "live, learn, work, play, farm" and not "live here, learn there and work elsewhere".

We thus propose labelling the demolition and rebuilding of HDB towns as "Regen" strategy (short for regeneration and consistent with the terminology used in other countries). As a country, we will benefit from new asset-types and new technologies built into each Regen town. If we parcelled out the work across the 25 or so HDB towns, there will be a new Regen town project taking off every four years.

The lease/sale of non-residential spaces in Regen towns provides attractive revenue streams which will help significantly defray the rebuilding costs. Each Regen project, with mixed-use assets catering to "live, learn, work, play, farm" and incorporating the latest technologies will lead to higher asset utilization and improved land value. As a consequence, the value of Singapore's land reserves will grow when each Regen town is completed. Given our ageing population, we will also incorporate "heal" and "farm" into the urban regeneration plans.

The proposal is thus good for Singapore's macroeconomic strength. Even as we minimize the problem of retirement adequacy and the value of public housing for Singapore citizens, we also enhance the value of our national reserves.

At the same time, these proposals provide a way for upgrading and boosting productivity, innovative capacity and competitiveness by reconfiguring Singapore's urban infrastructure towards a smart country. Singapore could be the only country in the world capable of upgrading and integrating the latest Information Technology, schools, intelligent offices, factories and homes and transport systems over the course of each century.

One way of envisioning this is Prof Tay Kheng Soon's proposal to use this continuous rebuilding to transform Singapore into what he terms a "Tropical Renaissance City". (Readers may refer to Annex 4 for more details.)

Section 5: Programme Costs and Fiscal Sustainability

While the cost of this programme will be large over the long term, we believe it is affordable and sustainable when amortized over 100 years, much the same way our similarly large 50-100 year investment to safeguard Singapore against climate change can be sustainably and responsibly financed.

The construction costs of a new flat are estimated to be around $180 psf. A standard 4-room 1,000 sqft flat would thus cost maximally $200,000 on average to demolish and rebuild. The current cost of replacing the entire stock of around 1.1 million HDB flats over the next 90-100 years (starting in 40-50 years with the oldest flats) is thus around $170-210 billion. [Note: more than three quarters of the total stock of flats are 4-room or smaller.]

Amortized over 100 years, this cost works out to an outlay, at present value, of around $1.5-$2.0 billion annually or around 0.3-0.4% of GDP today, allowing for a 2-3% inflation in construction costs. Additionally, being a massive long-term national programme, there would necessarily be economies of scale with bulk buying, hedging forward contracts, etc.

This yearly average budgetary cost of around $1.5-$2.0 billion can appropriately be set aside as a "sinking fund" annual payment underwritten and spent by the Government to continually rebuild and regenerate all HDB flats under its custody every 100 years.

Building costs are also unlikely to rise too steeply given prefab construction technology innovation and a shift towards high-density low-rise residences as opposed to the current low-density high-rise HDB precinct design. Both utilize the same land area but the former is more convivial socially and environmentally sensible. In fact, HDB construction costs have remained stable at around $150 psf over the last 10 years.[5] In the meantime, the long-term returns on investing the sinking fund before use by GIC, which makes a return of 3-4% above inflation, should ensure that the funding cost of this rebuilding programme remains affordably low relative to the Government's overall annual budget.

In theory, there is no reason why this lease renewal and rebuilding cycle cannot go on perpetually every subsequent 100 years since the cost of rebuilding can be sustainably included in recurrent Government investment expenditures given its affordable yearly cost relative to the growth and size of the State's fiscal reserves and resources.

In this regard, it is well established by the IMF that we have a structural fiscal budget surplus of around 4-5% of GDP and that we will still grow our reserves significantly through such surpluses as well as the currently unused, reinvested net investment income worth 1.5-2.5% of GDP over the coming decades. Reserves are also likely to grow even further because of high household savings and net structural long-term balance of payments inflows which are expected to persist for at least the next decade or two.

---

5 Cost estimates from Arcadis Construction Cost Handbook 2019 - Singapore

Fiscal Sustainability

The IMF estimates that we have a 4-5% of GDP structural budget surplus, of which around 2% is revenue from government land sales to the private sector which is renewed after the 30-99 year leases expire and which thus form recurrent sustainable revenues. Less conservative accounting (for e.g. amortizing investment properly) can yield another 0.5-1% of GDP).

In addition, we currently use only half of the net investment return contributions (NIRC) available from our reserves, leaving at least 2-3% of GDP currently reinvested in reserves. It may not be rational to save as much as half our long term real investment returns on reserves for future generations who are likely to be much richer when we can use it be for budgetary spending over the next 10-20 years when the bulk of our retired baby boomers are living out their final years and we are thus likely to need it the most. Future NIRC is also likely to be higher than current as our reserves are growing rapidly from strong national savings and long term capital inflows, not just from investment income.

We should, therefore, still have at least 6-7% of GDP left as a sustainable fiscal resource in the medium to long term, even after utilising only about half the remaining NIRC which should be sufficient to fund basic but increasing spending in healthcare, education and social security.

The leasehold reform in the HDB sector set out in this paper, therefore, does not adversely impact our current operating budget surplus as it is essentially redistributing the capital gains [which now reside in our reserves] into the value of old HDB estate back to HDB owners.

The total cost of rebuilding is also likely to stabilize and only grow modestly starting with the next 100 year rebuilding cycle as the citizen population stabilizes and the numbers of new flats similarly stabilize or shrink (though its composition may shift over time to larger flats as incomes rise) as the demographic profile combined with low citizen replacement rates suggest (See chart in Annex 2). Hence, it is unlikely that substantial new land acquisition will be needed for housing as it can come out of existing land banks. Hence, the lack of land to support these proposals is not likely to be a physical constraint.

Please see: https://www.edgeprop.sg/property-news/no-lack-space-10-million-population

While the long-term total cost of implementing our proposals is substantial, it is essential to keep in mind that spending around $1.5-2 billion annually or 0.3-0.4% of GDP of this ample fiscal headroom will not only help secure HDB owners' net asset values for themselves and their children, but also result in the entire HDB housing stock being rebuilt to state-of-art housing design standards and quality every century. This would be a feat of public housing and renewal unparalleled anywhere in the world. The ratio of social benefit to fiscal costs would thus be extremely high.

Alternatively, the cost of this programme may also be funded using a fraction of the funds from Government land sales which average around $7 billion or about 2% of annual GDP (reference Government Land Sales programme from 2011-2018).

Expenditure for this rebuilding programme is thus eminently affordable and should still leave considerable budgetary resources available to fund most other key long-term public expenditure needs like healthcare, an improved education system and better social security (See more detailed discussion in "Fiscal Sustainability" box story).

Section 6: Proposed Solution to Affordability of HDB Flats
Affordability of new BTO flats

In the same fashion, the Government can comfortably afford to reduce the current price of BTO HDB flats so as to reduce the average loan payback period to an affordable 10-15 years from the current 25 years. This is because construction costs merely represent 50% or less of the total costs as the State already owns the land which was acquired at much lower historical, often compulsory acquisition prices which are sunk costs to the Government. Therefore, the current overall fiscal cost is minimal.

In order to keep low-priced BTO prices from pulling down HDB resale prices, we propose that the HDB should extend the restrictions on market sale of BTO flats to 15 years' minimum occupancy period (MOP) for first-time buyers. Additionally, family units should only be allowed to own one low-priced BTO flat at any time. However, should they wish to upgrade to larger flats within the 10-15 year period, they should have the option to resell their flat to HDB at prevailing costs and purchase the larger desired low-priced BTO flat from HDB. The maximum MOP for the upgrading buyer should be 10 years if they upgrade after five years after their initial BTO purchase.

Our proposal, therefore, preserves a 15-year illiquidity discount between BTO flats and equivalent older resale flats. Added to the current location choice premium and the immediacy of purchase premiums, a stable equilibrium 50-60% discount between new low-priced BTO flats and more expensive, older resale flats should be able to be preserved over the long term.

These price premiums protect the current owners of HDB resale flats from losing capital value and at the same time ensure that their children as well as new first time buyers can still afford much cheaper new BTO flats with a lower 10-15 year loan repayment period. In short, our proposal, while benefiting new BTO purchasers, is unlikely to destabilise the current HDB resale market.

Using our assumption of $150-$200 psf building costs for example, a new 1,000 sqft 4-room BTO flat should only cost new buyers around $150,000-$200,000. A new 3-room BTO of 700 sqft should cost $110,000-$140,000 while a new 5-room BTO 1,300 sqft flat will cost around $210,000-$260,000. Some variation should be allowed for location differences. Since land value is no longer a factor in pricing, a simple markup formula can be adopted whereby outlying areas have zero markup, intermediate areas a moderate markup and good areas a higher markup and perhaps even also a longer lockup period before resale.

One huge benefit of these significantly lower BTO prices for new buyers will be the ability to save much more for retirement adequacy, education, healthcare or capital that can be used for entrepreneurial activity, which is currently tied up in the costs of more expensive HDB flats. The benefit of owning BTO flats at construction costs should, in our view, also extend to singles and divorcees.

Downgrading eligibility after retirement - a final boost to retirement adequacy

In the above proposals, every citizen is only entitled to one HDB purchase of cost-priced BTO flats per family unit, which can be sold in the resale market only after a 10-15 year holding period.

However, we also propose that a flat owner after age 65 should be eligible to sell his flat and downgrade to buy a smaller flat sold by HDB at cost. This enables the flat owner to maximise the capital value of his flat for retirement purposes from age 65 till death. Such low-cost BTO retirement flats can only be sold back to the HDB at "cost plus nominal economic growth minus depreciation" and cannot be sold by the owner in the resale market a second time no matter how long they live. The flat can then eventually be renovated by HDB and sold to other buyers.

HDB should further enhance this retirement-cash-out option by building many more low-cost studio flats for elderly couples or singles at cost. To make them more popular, these can be inserted in the spaces in existing estates in void decks or between blocks to enable ageing in situ so as not to disrupt social networks, preserve location familiarity and ensure the elderly are not isolated but supported by the rest of the community (please see research by Tay Kheng Soon, Singapore Version 2.0, Ageing In Place: https://youtu. be/JjlGE2VfA_I)

This downgrading eligibility to buy a smaller, low cost flat at cost will help fund the retirement of a rapidly ageing population with increasing life expectancy that may in future extend much longer than the current 85 years.

Proposed Solution to unaffordability of home ownership for the poor
In addition to the above proposals, HDB should ensure a sufficient stock of transparently means-tested, affordable, good quality subsidized low-rental flats for the bottom 30% of income earners with security of tenure.

In the increasingly unstable gig economy of the future with a much higher likelihood of technology-disrupted unemployment, it is unlikely that many of the bottom 30% of income earners will have sufficiently secure long term employment to afford and service a mortgage even for 10 years. This proposal, therefore, provides a safety net for their housing needs, which is severely under-provided for, given the current sacred cow status of ownership in public housing.

Section 7: Conclusion

These four major proposals of: (1) affordable 99-year lease top-up after 50 years, (2) state-funded rebuilding after 100 years, (3) BTO and retirement flat prices close to construction costs and (4) sufficient decent-sized and affordable rental flats, would collectively address the major problems of public housing by providing security of tenure, stable asset values and retirement adequacy for the majority of our population.

At the same time, it will help sustain affordable, high quality housing for future generations of citizens and HDB owners. This would result in lower unnecessary investments in unproductive capital, leading to more buoyant growth from higher household consumption and both public and private investments. Importantly, it will also provide a decent and affordable safety net of affordable rental housing for the poorer and less income-stable part of the population that is likely to structurally form a permanent feature of the future labour market.

Additionally, renewing the HDB housing stock every 100 years will ensure that the most modern and convivial design of integrated townships is available to Singapore citizens and existing HDB owners in perpetuity for generations to come. While the total cost is large, the annual cost is fiscally very affordable and would amount to a sustainable recurrent investment in the economic security, well-being and prosperity of our citizens, unequalled anywhere else in the world.

The combination of these enormous public housing benefits available only to citizens would provide Singaporeans with a more tangible basis to value their rights and privileges as citizens in a way no other country will be able to do.

As a nation, we can comfortably afford these reforms principally because, firstly, the Government owns the freehold rights to over

90% of land through past compulsory acquisition. Secondly, our large structural fiscal surpluses and strong reserve management capability makes these proposals eminently affordable and fiscally sustainable. Finally, HDB has developed the valuable capacity and capability to build, manage, retrofit and develop large, high-quality integrated-facility towns for the bulk of our citizens.

In the face of growing retirement inadequacy with a rapidly ageing population, increasing economic and employment uncertainty as well as inherently expensive housing due to our limited land size, it is time we capitalise on these fiscal, public land ownership and organizational strengths to reform out-dated parts of public housing policy so that public housing may achieve its full potential for the common good. It would truly represent a new milestone in attaining prosperity and progress for our people. Singapore will be a pioneer that other nations emulate.

Annex 1: Leasehold Extension Pricing and Practice

In theory, a market-based determination of the cost of topping up a 50-year-old property back to 99 years based on current public sector practice can be inferred from the "Bala's Table", which is used by the SLA and HDB to determine the pricing of a declining lease in a 99-year lease term property (chart form below).

Fig. 4: SLA Leasehold Table in chart form showing leasehold values as a percentage of freehold value

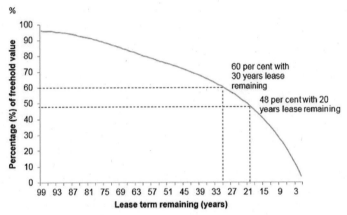

Source: Christopher Gee, https://www.todayonline.com/commentary/why-hdb-owners-should-forget-about-getting-windfall-vers

It can be seen from the chart below that using this accepted methodology as a guide for calculating lease values over the term of a 99-year lease, the 99-year lease loses around 20% in value after 50-60 years. The implied "fair value" of a lease top-up after 50 years is thus around 20% of the resale value of the flat (approximate figures are used to take into account the significant variation in using an appropriate discount rate of around 3.5%).

Fig. 5: Percentage Leasehold Value Comparison (PVIF discounted at 3.5% versus Leasehold Table)

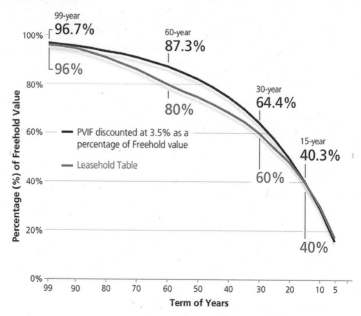

Source: Centre for Liveable Cities, https://www.clc.gov.sg/docs/default-source/commentaries/balas-table.pdf

This forms a theoretical market-based starting point accepted by local authorities for lease valuation. However, various countries with major similar international property markets like London often charge a little less for lease renewal ranging from 12-13% of the then value of the property to extend a 60-year-old lease by 90 years and around 15% for a similar extension to a 50-year-old lease This offers a price of around 15% to extend the lease of a 50-year-old property by 90 years as a lower alternative reasonable benchmark used in an established property market for setting base lease renewal prices.

Fig. 6: Typical cost to extend lease on £200,000 flat by 90 years

LEASE LENGTH	EXTENSION COST	PROFESSIONAL FEES (1)	TOTAL	POTENTIAL ADDED VALUE (2)
95 years	£5,000	£2,500	£7,500	£5,000
85 years	£6,000	£2,500	£8,500	£10,000
79 years	£8,500	£2,500	£10,500	£16,000
70 years	£14,000	£2,500	£16,500	£26,000
60 years	£24,000	£2,500	£26,500	£38,000

Typical cost to add 90 years to a lease, cost based on Leasehold Advisory Service data. Costs are per flat and can vary dramatically. Based on a £200,000 flat (£200,000 is its value with 999 year lease) with £200 annual ground rent. 1) This includes the valuation fee and freeholder's legal costs. 2) Estimates by Kinleigh Folkard &

Singapore is not alone in grappling with this thorny issue of renewing state-owned leases. China has a 70-year leasehold system and is drafting laws to allow leases to be renewed unconditionally. Hong Kong has automatically extended leases on some old properties, subject to an annual rent. Both of these major Asian economies' leasehold renewal processes and pricing are far more generous than our proposal or the UKs. Please see: https://www.scmp.com/week-asia/politics/article/2160662/singapores-homeowners-have-99-problems-and-their-lease-no-1

In short, the decision on leasehold renewal pricing is essentially a policy decision made for the greatest national benefit and while it should not be arbitrary or subject to populist pressures, it should be made with the welfare of the majority and economy foremost in mind rather than relying purely on market forces.

We therefore propose that for public housing in Singapore, 15% of the property value be used as a base 50-year extension price, to be discounted first by dividing an average plot ratio of 2.5 and second a further 50% discount to take into account mortgage financing and en bloc sale restrictions and encumbrances. The guideline price of lease renewal of 15% should thus be divided by a cumulative factor of 5 to give a guideline lease renewal price of around 3% of the value of the HDB flat.

It should be kept in mind that this proposed price is only a rough guideline, which has a defensible market-based derivation and is in line with established international precedent. As with social goods like education or healthcare, we believe it is incumbent on the Government to make the guideline price for lease renewal affordable to all citizens by further subsidies, as it currently does for upgrading. We therefore also recommend that this lease renewal price be repayable, interest-free over 10-15 years and be further subsidised up to 90% on a means-tested, case-by-case basis where necessary.

While acknowledging that public housing has become a de-facto store of life savings for much of our population, we also need to recognise that public housing in Singapore is fundamentally a social good and should not be determined, wholly or principally, on market asset-pricing measures.

Annex 2: Analysis of Risks of Housing Market Destabilization

The risks of destabilizing impacts on existing home prices due to the recommended reforms could present themselves in one of the following ways:

HDB resale prices surge unsustainably, as the effective lease increases for existing flats and the guaranteed renewal and rebuilding regulations boost their market value.

Resale prices could fall significantly as much lower-priced BTO flats pull down their values. Private housing prices could fall sharply as HDB property becomes much more affordable and attractive.

In general, we assess that the risks of an upside bubble in the form of a HDB resale price surge are low.

Firstly, while there will be a one-off jump in HDB resale prices effectively pricing in the prospect of fresh 99-year leases and guaranteed free rebuilding, this price jump will be capped by the limited total demand for HDB flats, which will likely be restricted largely to citizens as PRs will not be eligible for subsidized lease renewal or free rebuilding costs. If necessary, policy restrictions on PRs buying resale flats can be increased to further cap excessive increases in resale prices. Furthermore, the poorer physical condition of old flats would dampen both their resale and rental value, even after lease extension.

In addition, the long-term fundamentals for HDB resale flat prices are soft given that the local citizen population is shrinking demographically and that over the long term (about 15 years later) a steady stream of many low-priced BTO flats will qualify for resale. Old flats will also suffer from a depreciation and ageing effect despite renewed leases and guaranteed rebuilding.

Overall therefore, we do not expect a bubble to build up in HBD resale prices.

Similarly, the upside for private housing is limited both given current property market curbs and the competition from newly-reformed and more attractive HDB resale flats. If necessary, private property market curbs can be tightened should there be a surge in private home prices.

Turning then to downside property market risks, resale HDB prices should not fall sharply as the new cheaper BTO flats should be effectively segmented from the resale market by the new 15-year minimum lock-in period, the lack of choice in location and the normal 2-3 year queue and construction lead time. If necessary, restrictions on PR ownership of resale flats can also be relaxed to shore up demand.

Private property downside risks can similarly be prevented, if necessary, by relaxation of current property cooling measures.

In conclusion, excessive increases or falls in both private and HDB resale prices are not expected to happen through a combination of market fundamentals and relaxation or tightening of available policy tools.

Over the much longer term (30-40 years) shrinking demographic replacement rates may put pressure on old flat prices as baby boomers are replaced by smaller cohorts, although this should be ameliorated by the corresponding demand from PRs and new citizens (chart below).

Fig. 7: Asset valuation on the face of aging population

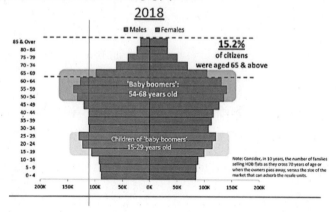

| THE FUTURE OF REAL ESTATE

Annex 3: Two Common HDB Stories
Case 1:

Mr Lim (67) and Mrs Lim (66) live in a 4-room flat in Hougang which is 35 years old, i.e. 64 years left on the lease.

Mr Lim is retired while Mrs Lim works in the security industry. Their HDB flat has been paid largely via Mrs Lim's CPF. Mr Lim has a few thousand dollars in his CPF.

They are concerned that their retirement savings might diminish along with the declining value for old flats. Since their son has gotten married and moved out, they can downsize to a 3-room flat which has a lower value (hence a smaller decline in future value).

The flat is worth $400,000 and the sales proceeds, net of fees and other expenses will be about $390,000.

The funds flow goes like this:

$170,000 of CPF money used for paying for the flat and interest expenses will be refunded to Mrs Lim's CPF Retirement Account. In addition, another $75,000 of unearned interest will be paid into her CPF Retirement Account.

The remaining $390,000 - $170,000 - $75,000 = $145,000 cash proceeds will go to their bank accounts. Out of the $245,000 that went back to Mrs Lim's CPF Retirement Account, $110,000 was retained as the minimum sum for Full Retirement Sum (FRS) and CPF will pay out a refund of $245,000 - $110,000 = $135,000 to Mrs Lim.

So Mr and Mrs Lim has $145,000 + $135,000 = $280,000 of cash and Mrs Lim has a Full Retirement Sum which will pay her about $1200 per month until she is 85 years old.

This sum of money is hardly sufficient for retirement as each of them have another 18-20 years (Life expectancy at age 65 is 19.1 years for males and 22.5 years for females). The cash is insufficient for the couple's living expenses of around $2000 per month as well as market rents of about $1700 for a 3-room flat if any bouts of illness strikes or if Mrs Lim loses her job or goes into retirement.

They thus want to use the $280,000 of cash and Mrs Lim can apply half of her CPF FRS (about $60,000) to buy a 3-room flat. Half of the FRS can be used, so the CPF Retirement Account is left with a Basic Retirement Sum (BRS) and that will pay out about $800 a month till Mrs Lim is 85. This is well below the $2000 needed for dignified retirement as a couple.

So they will purchase a 3-room flat at about $320,000 (taking into account expenses required for relocation, legal, valuation and agents fees). At their age and income level, they are not eligible for loans.

Ownership of a 3-room flat comes with additional expenses such as S&CC (Service & Conservancy Charges), property tax, etc. This means that Mrs Lim has to continue working well beyond the retirement age. And neither of them can fall ill. Life is tough.

If our proposals were enacted, first the 4-room flat they own would hold its value even if it was much older. Second, Mr and Mrs Lim could now at 65 downsize to a 3-room BTO at cost of $130,000 instead of a resale 3-room flat at $320,000. This would give them a cash savings of $150,000 after buying their smaller retirement flat. They could then buy another CPF LIFE of $1,200 per month, making their total retirement income $2,400 per month, significantly above the $2,000 dignified retirement level. They would still have $30,000 cash in case of any unexpected medical expenses or emergencies. Not so tough now.

Case 2:

Rafi (61) and his wife Siti (60) do not think they can retire.

11 years ago Rafi purchased a 3-room flat in Block 61, Lorong 5 Toa Payoh for about $200,000. He took a 20-year loan of $120,000.

This block's lease started on 01Jun1967 and the flat is about 53 years old, with a remaining lease of 46 years and 7 months.

Rafi is a chauffeur and a part-time car jockey. Siti is a homemaker and earns some occasional income baking and selling cakes from home. Rafi's CPF Retirement Account has about $40,000 and Siti's has about $10,000.

In 4 years' time, when Rafi turns 65, he will be paid around $200 a month from his CPF Retirement Account until age 90. Siti will be able to receive about $50 a month from her CPF Retirement Account in five years' time. These pay outs are barely enough for them.

Rafi and Siti have a home loan with a monthly mortgage commitment of about $600 till year 2028 when Rafi turns 70 years old.

Both spend about $300 a month on their utilities, telephone bills and S&CC. Food, transport and a bare minimum of day-to-day living will cost the couple another $600 a month.

They need about $1,500 a month, including their mortgage payment.

And yet their home value keeps dropping. By the year 2028 when he has fully paid the home loan, the flat's value is likely to have dropped to lower than $200,000. This is because the flat will be left with 37 years of lease at that time and whoever buys from him will have to use a large proportion of cash as they will face restrictions in financing their purchase with CPF money or bank loans.

What options do they have?

a. Sell the flat now ($220,000) and rent: sales proceeds minus $60,000 loan principle = $160,000 out of which $100,000 of CPF and accrued interest back to CPF. They will have $60,000 in cash and Rafi's Retirement Account will have $140,000 which will pay him about $700 a month after he turns 65.

b. Sell the flat later. They will continue to pay interest expenses for 9 more years, forego CPF interest and the value of the flat may decline $10,000 per year, shrinking their nest egg further.

c. Sell the flat and down-size to a 2-room flexi 40 years lease costing $60,000: they can use CPF but that means their cash of $60,000 and Rafi's Retirement Account of $80,000 will have to last them another 25 years.

d. Lease buy-back scheme: they can sell back 15 years of lease for (we are guessing here) $50,000 but all of that will go into Rafi's and Siti's Retirement Accounts and they will not have cash. After reaching 65, the monthly pay out to Rafi and Siti may be less than $500 a month.

If our proposals were enacted, Rafi will be less concerned about the declining value of his flat and he can then sell the flat and given the couple's retirement, opt to rent the low-cost flats from HDB using the proceeds from the sale. In another 5-10 years if he sells the flat, he will have $80-100k in net savings which can get him an annuity of $1,200 which is closer to the $2,000 poverty line for a couple. If the couple received $300 under the existing silver support scheme for elderly poor, their total income will be $1,500, much closer to a dignified retirement adequacy for him and his wife than without our recommendations.

Annex 4: Transforming Singapore into a Tropical Renaissance City

The present challenge is to protect the declining asset value of existing HDB flat owners while at the same time offer new BTO flats priced at $180psf, based only on construction cost. Taken together as described earlier, the two proposals render citizenship meaningfully tangible. While this is the immediate concern, it plays a catalytic role in eventually transforming the entire island into an Intelligent City. Land economics and social equity creatively visioned can transform this Island City State into a front runner in the race towards eco-sustainability but it starts with seemingly tiny but vital steps that cumulatively, guided by vision, can be transformative.

The forgoing of land price of the new BTO flats can be compensated by additional commercial plot ratio. The State can thus recover land value from this. But the increase in plot ratio requires a new kind of design with housing above and a mixed-use commercial podium below. This new model moreover also results in a huge increase in efficient use of land. The aggregated amount of useless fringe land normally to keep buildings apart is no longer required with a linear podium design. The aggregated useless land can now be returned to nature for parks and nature reserves.

Rebuilding after 100 years, of all flats, neighbourhoods and townships is necessary as this is the design life-span of reinforced concrete structures. This new urban model visualised as a climate adapted and energy efficient system is to **live, learn, work, play, farm and heal,** reducing the need to travel and be information-rich therefore with built-in intelligence. It has thus to be intentionally planned so that as people go about the routines of everyday life, going to school, to market, to shop, to work and to civic facilities etc., they naturally meet new people, are exposed to new ideas and information and experience new things, they thus gain knowledge experientially. This is the intelligent city to be aimed at, even while addressing the vexing housing questions.

Thus we imagine a super-convenient way of life provided by a multi-level, mixed-use podium that serves as main and secondary information arteries around which to live. This linear podium linked together becomes a neighbourhood, then more neighbourhoods eventually become a township and finally through elevated link-ways endowed with civic, educational and cultural facilities, the whole island becomes an intelligent island.

The continuous podium rooftop is the linear community garden for the housing above and below, commercial facilities, work places, tertiary institutions, shopping malls, robotic production units, urban farms, schools, restaurants, food malls, community clinics, entertainment places, etc. Life is thus freed from congestion stress. Robotic taxis, buses and the MRT provide transport to more distant locations if needed; otherwise, everything is only a short distance away from where one lives. Pedestrian paths, tracks for bicycles and PMDs provide access to last-mile destinations.

Like a three-dimensional vertical and horizontal web akin to the neurons, axons and synapses of the brain that will ultimately link the entire island, Singapore will be transformed into the Metropolis imagined by Lee Kuan Yew to a whole new level as the World's first Tropical Renaissance City in which Machine intelligence is matched by the agency of Human intelligence.

The Greater Southern Waterfront (GSW) will be the locale to pioneer the new integrated urban model.

From the GSW, the HDB townships and neighbourhoods rebuilt piecemeal through SERS and VERS before the massive rebuilding of all flats as they approach their 100-year replacement age, the ideas developed in the GSW will then radiate outwards. The GSW will also become Asia's Campus City akin to Boston, USA attracting the best and brightest to live and learn and thus form lifelong friendships with our Singaporean students, thereby naturally fostering a regional future together.

General References

For current HDB BTO prices, please see: https://www.srx.com.sg/hdb/bto

For macroeconomic impacts and determinants of house prices in UK, please see: https://www.economicsonline.co.uk/Competitive_markets/The_housing_market.html

For a description of homelessness in Singapore, please see: https://socialspacemag.org/going-public-homelessness-in-a-nation-of-homeowners/

4. For information about HDB's Lease Buyback Scheme, please see: https://www.hdb.gov.sg/cs/infoweb/residential/living-in-an-hdb-flat/for-our-seniors/monetising-your-flat-for-retirement/lease-buyback-scheme

9. Additional Lifelines for the Decaying Values of Old HDB Flats?

Note: This chapter was written on 20 August 2018 as a commentary about the government's proposal for VERS and interim upgrading. This chapter was not published. More than two years later, details about VERS are still lacking.

The Prime Minister threw an additional lifeline to the growing pool of old HDB flats by announcing a new en bloc programme. In his speech at the National Day Rally 2018, he announced that the Housing & Development Board (HDB) will start working on a Voluntary Early Redevelopment Scheme, or VERS in short.

While details are being worked out, here is what we do know:

1. The scheme will only apply to HDB flats that are more than 70 years old, i.e. fewer than 29 years on the lease. HDB will determine the criteria for selecting precincts that are eligible for VERS and it is HDB's prerogative to select the precincts and the residents may vote on whether they would like to participate in VERS.

2. Though the scheme will begin in 20 years' time in 2038, HDB will deliberate on the rules for compensation and how the programme may be financed. Compensation will not be as generous as those for the Selective En bloc Redevelopment Scheme (SERS) given that these precincts do not have as high redevelopment potential as those that have undergone SERS.

For residents of old HDB flats who are concerned about the decaying value of HDB flats, this could not have been more opportune.

The market's unrealistic expectations of SERS is what caused the problem of high resale flat prices. Many parents of young adults are concerned that resale flat prices are unaffordable and out of reach for their children, while BTO launches may not offer flats within a comfortable distance for their families.

While the Minister for National Development has, in early 2017, taken pains to caution families to avoid over-paying for old flats and confirmed that the terminal value of the 99-years of lease is in fact zero, today's announcement of VERS will likely push the asking prices of resale HDB flats up a notch.

Most "sellers", or HDB flat lessees who wish to consider transferring their lease away, will immediately raise their asking prices because they believe that their old flats will have the best likelihood for VERS or SERS.

Before we get too excited over the prospects of VERS, let us remind ourselves that two decades is relatively far into the future. Many questions will need to be answered: the percentage of votes required from the residents, whether all precincts of more than 70 years of age are automatically eligible, how many times will this plan require modification in the next 20 years, etc., etc.

From a simplistic point of view, it would seem that all families in these old flats will vote for VERS if their precincts are selected. With 29 or fewer years left on the lease, most families will not be able to monetize their lifelong savings by selling the old flats. There will scarcely be any buyers for these old flats because CPF usage is not allowed and loans from HDB are only available for a few years, up till when the flat is left with 20 years of lease. Even if these old flats were upgraded in the just-announced Home Improvement Programme II, the flats' valuation is limited to the cumulative lease value of the next 29 years.

But if we were to take a leaf from the private residential en bloc book, we can see that a large proportion of those who DO NOT vote for the en bloc sales are the senior citizens and retirees. Some prefer to stay within familiar surroundings while many others with insufficient funds in their CPF Retirement Account find it untenable as they will not get any cash out of the sale. Whether VERS will be well supported when it is launched in 20 years' time depends very much on setting a low threshold for the percentage of votes required.

Looking from the angle of advancements in technology and urban planning, we might recommend that VERS be introduced 10 years from today for HDB flats that are 60 years or older. The use of autonomous vehicles, personal mobility devices and drone-taxis are expected to be widespread within the next 15 years. Bringing VERS forward by 10 years will allow us to shed legacy designs and concepts, allowing the redeveloped HDB estates to remain relevant in the future era of technology.

Flat values will drop to zero

Earlier in his speech, PM Lee explained the rationale for 99-year leases of HDB flats and the need to recycle land for our future generations. He reaffirmed the government's stand that HDB flats will be returned, with zero residual value, to the HDB after their 99-year leases have run out.

Following up on Prime Minister Lee's speech, Minister Lawrence Wong informed through his blogpost that the HDB will work with the Central Provident Fund (CPF) Board to relax the rules for the use of CPF to purchase old HDB flats. This will allow older flats access to a wider pool of buyers and will assuage the fears of the residents of old flats. Any relaxation of CPF rules will further boost resale prices of HDB flats. But as the terminal value at the end of 99 years is zero, these policies merely kick the proverbial can down to the next owner of the flat, who will face issues with rapidly declining values in a decade or two from now, a depreciation that also affects their CPF retirement funds.

Conclusion

I applaud the government's desire to plan far ahead for our housing needs. In view of the rapidly increasing retiree population, I wonder why we do not throttle up the construction of more homes for the elderly in precincts that they are familiar with instead.

With the announcement on VERS and relaxation of CPF rules, we avail ourselves additional lifelines for old flats. But, given our past experience with rehousing our elderly folk, many might consider staying in the flats until the full lease has expired and so the success of VERS is far from guaranteed. And the short-term uplift to resale flat prices might just transfer the pain of the decay-to-zero values of old HDB flats and CPF savings to our children and their children.

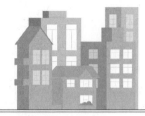

PART 3

PRIVATE RESIDENTIAL
AND EN BLOCS

10. Low Population Growth Leads to Low Property Values

First published on Storm-Asia.com, 18 April 2018

At the current pace that technology is disrupting every industry, changing the flow of work and squeezing more production out of assets in the sharing economy, the day of our reckoning seems near.

Soon, robots far more intelligent than humans will take away most of our livelihoods.

They are willing to work 24/7 and they do not ask for higher salaries, days off and engage in office politics. All that's needed is the occasional pampering — a few drops of oil and software upgrades will suffice.

Think driverless trucks, cashier-less stores, human-less bank branches and virtual schools.

What will the jobless people do? If we extrapolate the tech-disruption scenario further, we will come to a conclusion about the eventual rise of a "useless class" of humans. According to Professor Yuval Harari from the Hebrew University in Jerusalem:

"What we are talking about in the 21st century is the possibility that most humans will lose their economic and political value. They will become a kind of massive useless class — useless not from the viewpoint of their mother or of their children, useless from the viewpoint of the economic and military and political system. Once this happens, the system also loses the incentive to invest in human beings."

Professor Harari rose to prominence after his book *Sapiens: A Brief History of Humankind* was published in 2014. This and his second book *Homo Deus: A Brief History of Tomorrow* were both international bestsellers, including in Singapore. Industry leaders and heads of state have read and recommended his books. Microsoft founder Bill Gates wrote reviews in praise of both these books.

I reckon at least tens of thousands of people in Singapore would have read one or both books. But strangely, I do not see anyone warning about the impending net loss of jobs in Singapore.

While there are generous dollops of news served to us daily about tech disruptions and the urgent need for upgrading of skills to support multi-industry transformations, no one — not the media, not industry leaders and most worrisome, not policymakers — seems to acknowledge that more jobs will be lost than created. Maybe we are in denial. Or perhaps Singapore is an exception.

After all, we are a unique country that puts drivers back into driverless trains. So we do not have to worry about technology taking away our jobs.

Repercussions for Singapore

I believe that prospects of the future economy remain bright. The traditional measure of Gross Domestic Product can continue to show growth. However, that growth will be achieved despite a reduction in total employment. What worries me is that Singapore's policies, master plans and economic plans are premised on continued jobs growth and along with it, population growth.

The first signs of job losses are already obvious: in 2017 when GDP grew 3.6%, total employment excluding Foreign Domestic Workers shrank 0.3%.

In a scenario with a rising useless class, the following paragraph from the executive summary of the Population White Paper 2013 may probably be irrelevant sooner than we think:

"Up to 2020, if we can achieve 2% to 3% productivity growth per year (which is an ambitious stretch target), and maintain overall workforce growth at 1% to 2%, then we can get 3% to 5% Gross Domestic Product (GDP) growth on average."

Based on the assumptions of steady GDP growth and jobs growth, the Population White Paper 2013 estimated that our total population will reach 6.5 to 6.9 million by the year 2030, when about 2.5 million non-residents, mainly holding work passes, will reside in Singapore.

Back in 2012, perhaps the assumptions upon which the Population White Paper 2013 was built could not account for the disruptions we are facing now. However, the report by the Committee for the Future Economy published in early 2017 also failed to address the point that future economic growth will be "jobs negative".

We need to recognise that the relationships between GDP, labour force and productivity are losing relevance.

With so many changes reshaping the world, it may be time to realise that alternative methods of measuring a country's economic health and planning for the country's population should be considered.

Since 2006, the World Bank started to track the economic progress of countries by measuring their "wealth".[1] They believe that economic progress is better measured by including "assets such as infrastructure, forests, minerals, and human capital that produce GDP", especially in countries where policymakers are committed to building a sustainable future for their countries and for the world.

Some economists also measure economic progress by taking into account intangible traits, such as intellectual property and patents, brand value, workforce discipline and other environmental factors. These intangible parameters bring economic growth without the need for any increase in jobs.

Tough targets to meet

As I continue with researching for my next book about technology disruptions in the real estate market, I am convinced that even if our GDP growth targets are met, we will NOT get close to the lower end 6.5 million population in the year 2030.

Like most countries, Singapore will face a net loss of jobs and it will take tremendous, possibly uneconomical, efforts to grow the population of Singapore.

Together with the impact of an ageing population and the increasing deaths of Singapore's baby boomers, it seems that our housing segment may be oversupplied.

However, despite warnings of jobs declines and the irreversible demographics of ageing, many Singaporeans harbour dreams of owning their homes and investing in more residences for their financial freedom.

---

1 "The Changing Wealth of Nations", The World Bank, 30 January 2018, https://www.
worldbank.org/en/news/infographic/2018/01/30/the-changing-wealth-of-nations

For those who really itch to buy another residential property for investment, consider these factors:

1. The tech-disruption of jobs results in fewer foreign workers who are the potential tenants and therefore rental income is likely to be unattractive
2. Investors who had their jobs disrupted may sell their investment properties which have no rental income

Gig-economy concerns

Tentative work arrangements and sporadic income streams for gig-economy workers might mean that the demand for co-living spaces, staying with parents, and long-term rentals by Singaporeans will grow. Generation Z might prefer to keep their budgets flexible so as to spend on activities that they believe are worthwhile and purposeful.

In the sharing economy, asset ownership is secondary.

For those who wish to buy a home for their own enjoyment, my advice is: get yourself a trustworthy agent to look for well-built, freehold properties in districts 9, 10 and 11.

11. Too Early to Celebrate the Residential Market Recovery?

Co-authored with Tong You Xin; first published on Storm-Asia.com, 30 January 2018

While the property price index is on the rise, and en bloc sale frenzy continues to be the hot topic, the figures don't make sense as underlying issues point towards a troubled industry as the private housing rental index continues to drop and the HDB resale index continues to slide.

While looking for good news in the property market, the limelight was trained on the 4th quarter 2017 private residential data which climbed for two straight quarters after almost four years of decline that started in late 2013.

The media and most market pundits are cheering this little bright spot, and news about the en bloc sale frenzy continues to fan the flames of the hot housing market.

Underlying weakness persists

However, some indicators relevant to the residential market, which do not seem to get published, actually point to weak residential market fundamentals:

1. Save for one quarter of zero growth, the private residential rental

index dropped for its 17th consecutive quarter. The number of vacant private residences and Executive Condominiums (ECs) remained consistently higher than 30,000 for the last two years.

2. In the public residential segment, the HDB resale index continued its drop, with a decline of 1.5% for the full year in 2017.

3. Population growth at 5,000 in 2017 is anaemic, a multi-year low. The Population in Brief 2017 report published by the Department of Statistics in September 2017 revealed that the net population increase of 5,000 was due to an increase of 32,200 residents (defined as Singaporeans and Singapore Permanent Residents) and a decrease of 27,300 foreigners, most of whom were holding work passes (as opposed to dependent passes and student passes).

A weak employment market caused a loss of foreign workers which resulted in the small population growth. These foreigners who hold work permits, S-Passes and Employment Passes rent private residences, HDB flats and dormitories. Therefore, the drop in foreigner numbers is consistent with the gradual decline in the rental market.

The 2017 issues of labour reports from the Ministry of Manpower and the Business Expectations Survey for the Manufacturing Sector by the Economic Development Board point to similar trends.

The decline in our foreigner population was largely attributed to the fall in the number of work permit holders, especially in the construction, marine and offshore engineering sectors.

The services sector, including professional services and financial services, also contributed to declines in the number of foreigners, including the higher-salaried Employment Pass holders.

The weak employment market and declining foreigner population may explain the continued drop in rentals of private residential and

HDB flats. Poor confidence in the jobs market could also be a factor that led to the continued drop in HDB resale prices.

Combining residential market data and population data

Prices in the private residential market were largely driven up in the last two quarters by developers' demand for land through the en bloc sales of old apartments. This resulted in a reduction in the supply of resale private apartments, which would explain why the private residential price index went up.

Up to this point, the housing data made sense.

However, if we look at the population numbers versus the occupancy of our homes, the data becomes confusing.

The table below shows how our population growth was accommodated by the increase in the number of occupied homes.

	Population increase	Increase in number of occupied private residential units	Increase in number of occupied EC units	Increase in number of HDB flats*
June 2013	86,700	9,760	7	7,887
June 2014	70,600	10,035	1,420	16,142
June 2015	65,300	16,723	2,699	27,985
June 2016	72,300	14,965	3,928	23,616
June 2017	5,000	18,810*	4,325*	24,863*

* Total increase in occupied dwelling units in 2017 = 47,998 units

** Data for HDB is valid as of 31March of each year. As the HDB does not publish vacancy data, and HDB has strict rules about occupation of flats and Minimum Occupation Periods, we assume that the vacancy of HDB flats is negligible. Therefore, the increase in number of HDB flats is approximately equal to the additional number of HDB units occupied by families.

Source: SingStat, URA, HDB, IPA

In the 12-month period to June 2013, the population increase of 86,700 was sufficiently accommodated by an increase of about 17,700 private residences, ECs and HDB flats combined.

However, in the year to June 2017, despite a low population growth of 5,000, the housing data shows that almost 48,000 more homes were occupied.

Some might argue that we are seeing a spike in new household formation leading to additional demand for homes. However, if real demand were so strong, why have rental prices continually declined since 2013 till now?

If the increase in 17,700 occupied homes in 2013 could account for a population increase of 86,700 people, who are the occupants of the 48,000 residential units in 2017 when the population increased by a mere 5,000?

Note: Since this article was published, data for the next 3 years till 2020 shows that the number of dwelling units increased by 83,100, exceeding the total population growth of 73,000. Thus rentals are more likely to trend down over the next few years.

12. Coping with En Bloc Fever

First published on Storm-Asia.com, 4 December 2017

It would seem the en bloc fever has returned. Or certainly the hype around it.

Whether you are for or against it, as a subsidiary proprietor (SP) or owner of a strata apartment unit, you should get involved by participating in all the meetings to understand the deal that is being put together.

In addition to being an active observer, as and when invited by the Sales Committee for updates and discussions, you could also engage in the process by exercising your rights as an SP.

You could participate in the vote to appoint an experienced property consultant and an experienced lawyer. Depending on the size and value of your condominium block, the current market fee for the property consultant and lawyer amounts to about 0.5-1.0% of the en bloc value.

Paying the property consultant and lawyer an attractive fee will motivate them to stretch themselves to secure interest from several credit-worthy developers to fight tooth-and-nail to make attractive price-offers for your en bloc sale.

During the previous en bloc wave 10 years ago, a handful of sales involving weak developers were aborted as they could not raise sufficient capital and loans to complete the transactions.

That proved quite disappointing, for all the hard work put into the process. Some of the SPs had even committed to purchasing their next homes before the en bloc deals were aborted.

Keep track of milestones

While the Sales Committee is going through the en bloc sales process, e.g. setting up the Extraordinary General Meeting (EGM), getting the signatures from the SPs, providing regular updates, etc., you might like to keep track of the milestones and timeline.

The en bloc process is strictly regulated and the rules have tightened over the years. This is to ensure that past mistakes are not repeated and that each en bloc sale takes into consideration the needs and the views of all SPs, dissenting ones included.

The powers and responsibilities of the Sales Committee and their members, the property consultant and the lawyer are well defined. The strict guidelines enhance transparency of the en bloc process, keeping everything above board for the SPs and the bidding developers to enter into the sale of the properties.

Crossing the finish line

When a qualified developer has made a bid at or above the reserve price, and the Sales Committee has agreed to accept the bid on behalf of the SPs, the transaction is considered done. Well, almost.

If less than 100% of the SPs agreed to the en bloc sale, the dissenting SPs are allowed to present their cases at the Strata Titles Board (STB). If the dissenting SPs have good reasons, such as if there were evidence to show that the Sales Committee did not abide by the correct procedures, the STB could stop the en bloc transaction from proceeding.

If the en bloc sale is given the go-ahead by the STB, the winning developer will likely allow you and your family at least six months to move out to your new home.

The six-month period is sufficient time for you to allocate your finances and find a comfortable home, be it rental or purchase.

Allocating the en bloc windfall

A part of your receipts might be used to pay off remaining bank loans and another significant sum will have to go into you and your spouse's CPF accounts. The rest of it will be cash in your bank accounts.

How you might want to allocate the cash and CPF monies to purchasing your next home will depend on your family's needs, your age, your lifestyle and perhaps your retirement plans.

You might consider renting a home while you take your time to look around for options, including overseas properties.

If you decided to buy another home and you need to take a bank loan, do note that there are restrictions depending on your age and the loan servicing capacity your current income allows you.

After all, we have all aged 10 years since the last en bloc wave and mortgage restrictions have tightened since.

Others may opt to purchase a smaller, lower-priced property without tapping on bank loans, just using cash and CPF funds. Those who opt to downsize your property and hold cash might even be in a position to enjoy semi-retirement and take that much dreamed about round-the-world trip!

Based on my observations, the profile of the recent en bloc beneficiaries are generally middle-aged or older, most of them will be purchasing smaller-sized properties with little, say $300,000, or no loans. They are likely to put aside some of their cash for their children and for their retirement.

Consider all options

As the private residential resale market seems to be hotter now, given the en bloc wave sweeping us, many will find that the asking prices in the resale market have gone up. However, HDB resale prices have been dropping gradually and for the retirement-minded en bloc sellers, moving into a HDB flat for retirement might be a financially prudent option.

It is essential for potential en bloc beneficiaries to carefully think through the next steps for yourselves and your loved ones.

With a clear idea of the en bloc process, you can begin speaking with trusted property advisors to consider your next move such that once the en bloc sale goes through, you can quickly put your plan into action!

13. Have En Bloc Sales Hit The Wall?

With research support from Justin Chong and Leonard Wee; first published on Storm-Asia.com, 27 February 2019

There are mixed sentiments about en bloc sales. There are those who wouldn't mind the extra cash that some of these en masse sales deliver, but there are those who are against the idea of being driven out of house and home and forced to hunt for a new home at today's prices.

The 80% buy in — 80% of strata area and 80% of share value — has generated much anguish and opportunity. It has freed up land and given developers another go at choice plots of land, while the government rubs its hands in anticipation of tax windfalls.

Despite the optimism held by many analysts and marketing agents, more than 30 en blocs have launched for sale since a year ago but have found no bidders. Several projects, such as Windy Heights, Park View Mansions, Gilstead Mansion, Margate Point and Spanish Village recently re-launched for sale at lower prices but still found no bidders. In contrast, the owners at Pine Grove, Mandarin Gardens and People's Park Centre seem supremely confident about the market, and have raised their asking prices.

I am of the opinion that the en bloc cycle has reached its end.

With a tepid population growth, rising interest rates, higher stamp duties and new limitations on residential developments, developers are loath to look at en bloc opportunities, unless something is available for sale at heavily discounted prices.

A weak start

The first three residential launches of 2019 probably set the tone for the residential market in 2019: lacklustre.

Based on developers' declarations to the Urban Redevelopment Authority (URA), Fourth Avenue Residences sold 74 units in January. Out of a total of 476 units, this new launch is 16% sold.

The other two launches in January registered similar results. Fyve Derbyshire reported 11 units sold, or 15% of a total of 71 units. RV Altitude reported 19 units sold, or 14% of the 140 units.

Some developers spin the narrative, claiming they merely released a small number of units for sale, resulting in a much higher "percentage sold" figure. Such was the case at The Woodleigh Residences, when after achieving 30 units out of a total 667 units in its sales launch weekend on 10 and 11 November 2018, the developer announced that "about 60% of 50 units released were sold".

The market had not been informed that the developer was only making 50 units available during the launch weekend. As earlier news articles had alluded to more than 2,000 visitors thronging the show flat on the first day of preview on 27 October 2018, I was led into thinking that most of the 667 units would be cleared when it opened for sale on 10 November.

Fig. 1 Percentage of units sold, versus the total number of available units, at new residential launches from August 2018 to January 2019.

Source: International Property Advisor, URA

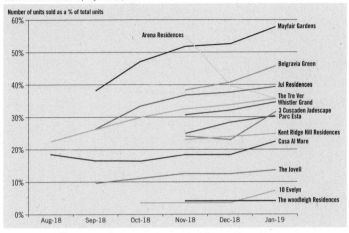

Fig. 2 Percentage of units sold versus the total number of available units, for Stirling Residences, Riverfront Residences and Park Colonial which all launched for sale within the hour of the announcement of cooling measures on 05 July 2018.

Source: International Property Advisor, URA

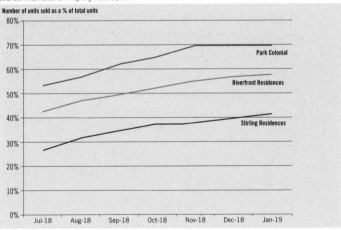

As of mid-February, the tally for The Woodleigh Residences: a cumulative 27 units, or 4% of 667 units, reported sold. In fact, sales numbers have declined since their statement to the press announcing their 60% sales rate.

Unsold stock building up

If we look at the results of the January 2019 launch projects from another angle, Fourth Avenue Residences has another 84%, or 402 units to sell, while Fyve Derbyshire has another 85% or 60 units to sell and RV Altitude has 86% or 121 more units to clear.

The Woodleigh Residences has 640 more units, or 96%, to sell.

In fact, post-July 2019 cooling measures, the pace of developers' sales has generally been slow beyond their initial launch.

Fig. 1 shows the projects that were launched after the cooling measures were imposed. Some projects showed declines in sales after their initial launch as buyer's remorse kicked in or the buyers did not want to proceed with the purchase. Some buyers may have backed out, hoping that lacklustre sales will result in a discounted price down the line.

Even the three projects that scrambled to launch on the fateful night the cooling measures were announced (Fig. 2) subsequently saw a slowdown in pace of sales, having to contend with fresh competition.

Developers feeling the heat?

In its February report, *Developers Pre-Sales: More than Meets the Eye*, Credit Suisse noted that several developers reported high number of units sold followed by a high number of returned units. The report suggested that several developers allowed multiple extensions of the exercise deadline for buyers' Options to Purchase in order to lock in the interest of buyers early and to prevent them from committing to other new launches. We cannot forecast if there will be more cancellations in the next few months.

According to the URA mid-month report for developers' sales, the total number of unsold residential units (excluding Executive Condominiums) increased from 11,148 in June 2018 to 16,938 units in January 2019. Now with a slew of new projects to launch and sales figures plateauing, the cumulative unsold stock is expected to grow.

Further pressured by rising interest rates, developers will have little choice but to focus all their energy on clearing stock.

The slow pace of sales and the intense competition are expected to worsen for developers in 2019. Based on land sales transacted in the en bloc market and the Government Land Sales programme, developers may release another 20,000 residential units across 50 new developments this year.

What hope for en bloc sales?

It is apparent that developers are less enthusiastic in land sales, and even less so in buying land through en bloc sales where the risks are higher. Following the cooling measures of July 2018, only two en bloc projects found buyers, while a developer backed out of another.

Notably, on separate occasions, Cheng Wai Keung, the chairman of Wing Tai Holdings, and Lee Chee Koon, the CEO of CapitaLand, told the media that they would refrain from participating in residential land acquisitions in Singapore until prices were attractively low and policy measures were more certain.

My advice to the en bloc hopefuls is to abandon the en bloc sales process. This will allow the serious sellers a chance to list their old properties in the resale market.

Hoping against hope and still being enslaved by the en bloc process will simply hinder the genuine and urgent sellers. And waiting longer will simply lead one into a market flooded with even more unsold residential units that are competing for attention from punters.

14. Sir James Dyson Sucking Up The Losses?

First published on Storm-Asia.com, 26 October 2020

About 15 months ago in July 2019, the real estate industry in Singapore was celebrating and trumpeting the sale of the largest non-landed residential property in Singapore — the triplex penthouse in Wallich Residence.

Developer Guocoland sold the penthouse for S$73.8 million, attractively discounted from a sticker price of $108 million.

The lucky buyer — none other than the high-profile Sir James Dyson, one of the richest Britons today. The ultra-secretive man whose name is attached to expensive bagless vacuum cleaners and hairdryers. And he wanted to build electric cars in Singapore.

The investment made waves in Singapore. It was hyped up in the local media and was earnestly dissected and discussed amongst property industry players. One could say it was the talk of the town.

The international media ensured the buzz spread to key cities such as London and Hong Kong.

By October 2019, the electric car idea had run flat.

And a year later, Singapore's *Business Times* revealed that Sir James had sold the globally famous penthouse for $62 million. In the midst of a viral pandemic that is in its third wave in many countries, a single dwelling transacted at a price of $62 million would catch most people's attention. More so if the seller had taken a capital loss of $11.8 million and an estimated total stamp duty bill plus agents' fees of more than $12 million.

An investment of $73.8 million that resulted in a loss of about $24 million after 15 months? That should easily make its way into real estate investment textbooks as a case example of 'What Not To Do'.

I am puzzled by this series of events

First off, the neighbour downstairs must be fuming. Just one floor below, apartment #61-01 was transacted in January 2020 for $4,987 psf.

Sir James' penthouse #62-01, which has 21,108.2 sqft of strata area, was sold at $2,937 psf, or 41% less.

My second concern has wider implications.

Taking a 16% loss on this penthouse over a 15-month period does not bode well for Singapore's reputation as a global financial hub for high net worth individuals and the private banking sector. Many observers brushed it off lightly, saying that this loss is no big deal to a multi-billionaire.

But does a multi-billionaire flush money down the toilet?

Prior to investing in the penthouse, was Sir James ill-advised by his financial planners and his property agents? Did his business run into deep trouble within the last 15 months such that he was no longer able to hold on to this internationally high-profile investment?

Would a person who is paid $200,000 a year, buy 10 packets of $4 chicken rice and then dump the 10 packets into the nearest rubbish bin simply because he can easily afford $40?

The third observation, based on comments from the market, suggests that Sir James might be able to write off the $24 million losses against his income taxes. If this were true, does it set an example for other ultra-high net worth Individuals who could similarly take advantage of Singapore's prime real estate, dumping them for significant losses (including hefty stamp duties) so that income taxes in their tax-resident countries may be reduced? Would such actions raise the ire of HM Revenue & Customs or other tax authorities?

Reputational risk

From a capital markets viewpoint, this example of value destruction is something that Singapore's reputation does not need.

Our real estate and finance industries pride ourselves as a preferred listing destination for Real Estate Investment Trusts (REITs), with more than 40 REITs listed on the Singapore Exchange, and counting. We can ill afford a billionaire Lord or Knight buying $100 million retail malls or office blocks and dumping them after a year for $30 million losses, to save on taxes or otherwise. The valuations of many assets in the small island of Singapore will be affected by such value-destructive actions.

While the authorities earnestly protect Singapore's real estate from speculative investors to prevent overheating and avoid property bubbles, we need to protect capital values from plunging due to the actions of speculative investors. Our reputation as a safe haven for real estate investors took decades to build. Real estate speculators who can afford to splurge on losses and on property taxes will dent our good reputation.

The last time an international high-flyer sold a penthouse with a big loss was billionaire Katsumi Tada from Japan. He took a $15.8 million loss on a 6,017 sqft penthouse at St Regis Residences in 2015, having held the investment for eight years across the Lehman Crisis. The stamp duties paid were less than $1 million which meant that his total loss was $16.8 million.

An investment holding period of eight years is reasonable in real estate circles and within that time frame, Japan's fortunes changed for the better and his investment priorities could have shifted elsewhere.

In contrast, even though Sir James' spokesperson provided reassurances that he remains committed to investing in Singapore, the magnitude of a $24 million loss over a 15-month period seems colossal.

But wait. Do we know that Sir James actually lost money in this deal?

I am unable to find any articles that quoted the buyer, the seller, the agents or anyone involved in the transaction that the purchase price was indeed $73.8mil.

There was also no price data for the transaction of this 62nd floor penthouse in REALIS, the Urban Redevelopment Authority's database. Most of the news articles in Singapore and across the globe can be traced back to the *Business Times* article which stated "BT understands…" without being able to confirm the purchase price.[1]

---

1 Kalpana Rashiwala, "Dyson owner forks out S$73.8m for Singapore's costliest penthouse", The Business Times, 10 July 2019, https://www.businesstimes.com.sg/real-estate/dyson-owner-forks-out-s738m-for-singapores-costliest-penthouse

We do know from REALIS and caveats filed on this property, that the apartment was sold for $62 million.

Is there a possibility that Sir James purchased the penthouse for at a much sweeter price than $73.8 million and therefore, he did not lose $24 million? However, neither Sir James nor his spokespeople confirmed or denied that he took a massive loss on this short-term property play.

In any case, with this supposed $24 million loss on the penthouse coming a year after his electric vehicles venture was scrapped with over $300 million written off,[2] what Sir James has signalled is that his investment managers might need to relook their real estate strategy. Or perhaps that he needs the services of a solid team of real estate advisors.

---

2 "Dyson has scrapped its electric car project", BBC News, 11 October 2019, https://www.bbc.com/news/business-50004184

PART 4

COMMERCIAL (OFFICE & RETAIL) AND INDUSTRIAL

15. Co-working Space — Still Cool to Hot Desk?

Co-authored with Hazel Tan; first published on Storm-Asia.com, 6 August 2018

The impact of the noisy minority is something to keep in mind with all the noise being made about the rise of the commercial property sector.

Advertisements shouting "No Additional Buyer Stamp Duty!" and no onerous restrictions on loans will entice property investors to cross over from the residential market to the office market.

For the past year, most industry watchers have upgraded the Singapore office market to a buy, asserting that office rentals and office demand have turned the corner to clear blue skies and a rosy future.

But you may want to take a look at the bigger picture. Broad market data does not seem to back up this assertion. Vacancy rates hovering at the low teens in the past six quarters are at economic recession-levels last seen during the Lehman Crisis.

Dig deeper into the analysts' bullish forecasts and we realise that the forecasts are focused purely on the Grade A sub-segment of office space in the core Central Business District (CBD).

Fig. 1: Vacant Office Space and Vacancy Rate from 1Q 2007-2Q 2018

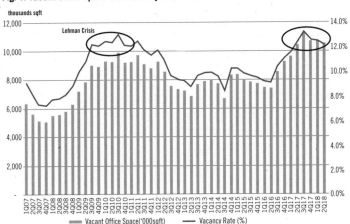

Vacant Office Space('000sqft) ▬▬ Vacancy Rate (%) ——

Lower grade offices and office buildings located outside the CBD may suffer from weak demand, falling rentals and high vacancies, but no one tracks their performance and so the layman will not get to read about their prognoses.

Rise of co-working spaces

A significant driver of office demand in the past two years came from co-working space operators.

In Singapore and the region, co-working spaces have proliferated, and is set to grow further. Giant private equity backed co-working space providers make for stunning headlines.

For example, WeWork plans to open one new office every three months over the next 18 months. JustCo is jointly investing US$177 million with Frasers Property and Singapore's Government Investment Corporation (GIC) to develop a co-working space platform across Asia.

Flexible workspaces embodies the transformation of the work environment, with increased opportunities for workers to interact, shared-spaces to innovate and having a sense of community in the workplace. It also promises a more economical way for small companies to operate, saving money on office costs and utilising resources more efficiently.

A strong push by the government for innovation and entrepreneurship, the millennial mindset which is more tuned to collaboration, and a proliferation of start-ups riding on multiple technology waves, led to this sub-segment of office space becoming trendy and hip.

Suddenly, the office environment has become livelier, as people get to meet other like-minded individuals and work together to brew and spawn new products and business ideas.

However, the co-working space concept has been around for decades. Its earliest version appeared in the guise of serviced offices with partitions and cubicles. It metamorphosed once during the dotcom boom era through business incubators and start-up accelerators. It recently morphed again, backed by heavy-weight venture money, with lots of hype, into open-plan layout offices hosting a range of occupiers who are members, rather than tenants, of the space.

How do co-working spaces affect the office market?

If the bulk of the increased demand for office space is attributed to the growth of co-working spaces, we should be more cautious about being overly optimistic that the office market is turning up.

A co-working space operator may lease an entire floor in an office tower of, say 15,000 sqft. This space is immediately available for sub-letting, sometimes as cubicles and desks, but most commonly in the form of "memberships" where members or subscribers are allowed to use the co-working space for certain hours over the membership period.

Since the space leased by co-working operators is almost immediately available for lease again, the "demand" for office space shown in office market reports do not reflect actual office-user demand.

We surveyed co-working spaces in Singapore and compiled the data from 2015 to 2017. The proportion of the increase in occupied office space contributed by co-working spaces has risen significantly: from 15% in 2015, to 64% in 2016 and to 75% in 2017.

Due to the efficiencies gained from the "time-sharing" element of co-working spaces, similar to car-sharing, bike-sharing and home sharing, a 15,000 sqft co-working space may house as many office users as 45,000 sqft of normal office space would.

Co-working space competes with, and cannibalises, normal office space.

And to complicate things further, there is no definition or data available for the utilisation rates or occupancy rates of co-working spaces. Therefore, we are unsure of the magnitude of the impact that co-working spaces have on the traditional office market segment

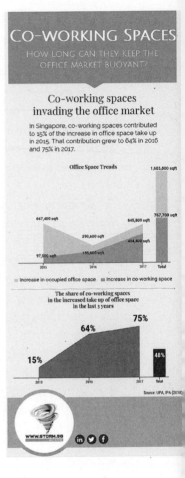

CO-WORKING SPACES
HOW LONG CAN THEY KEEP THE OFFICE MARKET BUOYANT?

Co-working spaces invading the office market

In Singapore, co-working spaces contributed to 15% of the increase in office space take up in 2015. That contribution grew to 64% in 2016 and 75% in 2017.

Office Space Trends

Increase in occupied office space   Increase in co-working space

The share of co-working spaces in the increased take up of office space in the last 3 years

Source: UPA, IPA (2018)

WWW.STORM.SG

Flexible workspaces beyond the office market

It seems that the competition facing traditional office spaces is not just coming from co-working space operators. Co-working space operators are also found outside areas designated for office use.

For example, the National Library Board has set up Smart Work Centres (SMCs) which are co-working spaces in public libraries. These SMC are pay-per-use workspaces that are fully equipped with meeting rooms, video-conferencing facilities, Wi-Fi and photocopiers.

The drop in retail rentals made it viable for co-working space operators to lease spaces in shopping malls, for example Trehaus at Claymore Connect and JustCo at Marina Square.

Co-working spaces are also found in spaces designated for use as Business Parks and Light Industries.

Flexible workspaces beyond co-working operators

Large corporations have also introduced their own concepts of communal working spaces in their offices, and have invited start-ups to join them to co-create and innovate new ideas and products. An example of this is Level 3 by The Unilever Foundry and Padang & Co, a co-working space that brings Unilever, start-ups and entrepreneurs together. This trend is expected to continue. Rather than signing up with co-working spaces, start-ups and small and medium-sized enterprises (SMEs) may work from such co-working spaces within the offices of large corporations.

This trend will have a small and negative impact on co-working space operators.

How will office landlords react?

Competition for SME tenants will be stiff since co-working space operators offer flexible and attractive lease terms with low upfront costs.

For investors of small office spaces looking for SME tenants, the information above is clear: the office segment is seeing recession-level vacancy rates and there does not seem to be light at the end of the tunnel for non-Grade A office space.

Perhaps lowering the asking rental, or quickly selling the office unit since the residential cooling measures might swing the less-informed investors to invest in office space, might be the way to go.

For owners of large buildings, several have already adopted the "if you can't beat them, lease to them, or form joint ventures with them" policy.

The top-tier co-working space operators offer lease terms that require landlords to cover the costs of interior renovations and to take a share of the revenue.

Discerning landlords know that most co-working space operators rely on venture capital money to keep their operations running. To anchor a global co-working space in a building by paying for interior renovations may be worth the landlords' risks. However for revenue sharing, landlords are uncertain about how much they will actually be paid. Co-working space operators sell "memberships" that allow subscribers to use their facilities at various locations across the world.

How will this revenue be shared?

Landlords who felt that they are getting a raw deal from co-working space operators have decided to go the joint venture route. That is not without risks, too. Some of the concerns include the quality of the transient tenants in co-working spaces and the credit standing of the co-working space operators (almost all are backed by venture capital and many will not make it to the next round of funding).

Seeing how flexible workspaces are not confined to just the office sector, or even to the locations from which they operate, and that large corporations are also creating their own versions of flexible workspaces, it would seem that the growth in demand in the office market may not last.

Furthermore, if we were to take a leaf from the books of the sharing-economy disruptors such as oBike and Uber, once a market is saturated, the pull-out will be fast and painful.

16. Three Pills for Singapore's Retail Ills

Co-authored with Brandan Koh and Hazel Tan; first published on Storm-Asia.com, 16 January 2020

Unless you are selling snacks laced with salted eggs, the business of doing retail in Singapore is tough. With a tiny domestic market, there are no "economies of scale" for retailers to leverage on. Marketers, analysts and economists often equate the 5.7 million population as the size of the consumer market. Or they might point to the high median household income of about S$9,300 per month and dream that consumers have strong spending power.

The real data is not so rosy

One million of the 5.7 million population are foreign domestic workers and work permit holders (such as those in the construction and waste management industries). A sizable proportion of the half million permanent residents do not live in Singapore even if they do make regular trips here. And while we have 1.32 million resident households, 160,000 households have no income or are retired.

The seemingly high median household income of S$9,300 per month is derived from 1.16 million households, skewed upwards by the many wealthy new citizens and new permanent residents.

The real addressable consumer market in Singapore is probably about 4 million individuals. Depending on the products and the location of the shops, some retailers may also consider their target market to include the transient 19 million foreign visitors, who stay three to four nights in Singapore, and the unknown millions of visitor-trips by Malaysians who cross the causeways.

Walking away

The recent decision by cosmetics retailer Sasa to withdraw from Singapore is just one of many pieces of evidence about the weak consumer demand. The 22 Sasa stores will be closed and about 170 employees will be affected. Sasa revealed that it suffered six consecutive years of losses despite efforts to turn its fortunes around.

Home-Fix, another household brand that many Singaporeans are familiar with, started 2019 with 11 stores but had closed all their stores by mid-December, marking a complete end to its bricks-and-mortar presence in Singapore.

The failing retail scene is not entirely the fault of the retailers failing to adapt to shifting consumer trends. Home-Fix was heralded by Prime Minister Lee Hsien Loong during the 2018 May Day Rally as a prime example of how retailers were responding to changing consumer preferences and technological disruptions by moving into services, providing experiences and doing online sales.

Nine months after Jewel Changi Airport opened, and claimed visitor numbers higher than the annual visitors to the Vatican Museum and Sentosa Island combined, retailers are already feeling the pain of sub-par sales.

There seems to be no escaping the ills of consumers tightening their belts. Total retail sales value has been dropping since mid-2018 even as population growth is still positive.

Fig. 1: Singapore Retail Sales (S$ Billions)

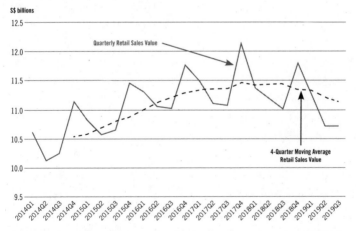

Singapore's consumers market value as seen from this graph of the Quarterly Retail Sales Value and the 4-Quarter Moving Average. The downward trend, apparent from mid-2018, looks set to continue into 2020. Source: Singstat, IPA

Tourist troubles

But what about the other part of the demand equation? Singapore has often touted tourist dollars as a significant source of income. Visitor arrivals have been growing significantly in the last three years – from 16.4 million in 2016 to 17.4 million in 2017 and 18.5 million in 2018. There is a possibility that visitor arrivals will exceed 19 million in 2019.

Sadly, despite higher headcount figures, tourism receipts in shopping and F&B are not growing. According to the Singapore Tourism Board, visitors spent $5.96 billion on shopping in 2016. This increased to $6.17 billion in 2017 and then dropped 13% to $5.39 billion in 2018. For F&B, receipts declined from S$2.79 billion in 2016 to S$2.65 billion in 2017 and S$2.59 billion in 2018. We believe that both numbers will drop further when data for 2019 is fully released.

It is worrisome that the record-breaking visitor arrivals in 2018 and 2019 could not prevent retail sales from declining.

Some signs of retail weakness were apparent long before. Due to an onslaught of new supply and stiff competition from e-commerce, shop rentals in the Central Area have dropped 18%, from a post-Lehman high of about $9.00 per sqft per month in early 2011, to S$7.32 per sqft per month in late 2019.

Vacant retail space increased over the past decade and hit a record high of 4.9 million sqft in 1Q 2019.

What might prevent the retail apocalypse? What do we do with all the space?

First recommendation: we need to shrink the total stock of retail space quickly, say by 20% of what we have today.

Fig. 2: Vacant Retail Floor Space (2014-2019)

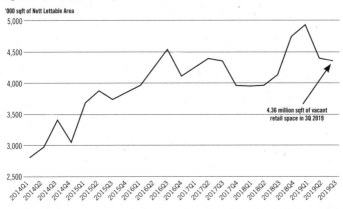

Vacant retail shops have been increasing against a backdrop of healthy economic growth in the last decade. Compounded by a decline in consumer spending, most landlords of retail shops are struggling for new ideas to make ends meet. Source: URA, IPA

It is not difficult to see why vacant space will keep increasing. As sure as video/DVD shops followed the way of the dodo, shops selling digital cameras, bank branches, bookstores, magazines and newsstands, etc., will be closing in significant numbers. We have previously stated that Orchard Road can be saved only if we stopped thinking of it as a retail street. It has lost the edge and it could do better with 20% of its space repositioned/renovated for medical, health and wellness services and 20% for educational services.

Secondly, let's not kid ourselves and recognise that creating experiential shopping, mining big data, offering omni-channel touchpoints and services or investing in digitalization (whatever that means) are merely short-term patches. Once a competitor, followed by another, starts to up the ante with services, experience and omni-channel offerings, everyone will be competing at the same level again.

Third recommendation: for all the billions that we poured into scientific research, creating intellectual property and filing patents, we should be spending at least a tenth of the billions in fashion, design and brands. Similar to sports, Singapore has the money to buy the talent, then quickly groom our own talent thereafter.

A distinct lack of local designer brands that are able to tango with international luxury brands means there is zero for anyone to buy as fashion items in Singapore. Fashionistas consider visits to Gucci's flagship store in Milan, Italy and Chanel's flagship store in Paris, France as making pilgrimages. Visiting the Orchard Road outlets of Gucci or Chanel is far from that.

A homegrown brand will be able to generate more organic growth for Orchard Road rather than importing the latest and greatest of Hermes and Louis Vuitton: let's face it, how often will the brand give Singapore the privilege of carrying an item that Paris, London, New York or Tokyo has yet to debut?

A massive investment towards building a range of local luxury fashion brands we are proud of is way overdue. And that just might be that last retail shot in the arm Orchard Road truly needs to cure its ills.

17. Empty Stores and Shopping Bags

First published on Storm-Asia.com, 4 February 2020

In doing my regular shopping mall surveys, my hopes were up in November and December 2019 that the shopping crowds may have improved, such that year-on-year performance of retail sales value could reverse from nine months of contraction.

According to the announcement by the Urban Redevelopment Authority (URA),[1] "Prices of retail space increased by 1.8% in 4th Quarter 2019, compared with the increase of 1.1% in the previous quarter. Rentals of retail space increased by 2.3% in 4th Quarter 2019, following the same increase of 2.3% in the previous quarter. For the whole of 2019, prices of retail space increased by 1.3%, compared with the increase of 0.6% in 2018; while rentals of retail space increased by 2.9%, compared with the decline of 1.0% in 2018."

But, I was wrong.

Who's spending?
What seemed to be larger crowds in the malls did not translate into higher retail sales in November 2019. The dollar value of retail sales dropped for the 10th consecutive month. The year-on-year sales

1 "Release of 4th Quarter 2019 real estate statistics", Urban Redevelopment Authority, 23 January 2020, https://www.ura.gov.sg/Corporate/Media-Room/Media-Releases/pr20-06

(excluding motor vehicles) dropped 0.6% with the biggest drops seen in the categories of "Furniture & Household Equipment" (-10.9%) and "Department Stores" (-8.4%).

According to Singstat, the total retail sales value in November 2019 was $3.6 billion, of which online sales made up 8.0%, or about $288 million, due to the major online shopping events such as Singles' Day and Black Friday.

On the bright side, Food & Beverage services revenue grew 5.5% y-o-y across all categories to reach a total value of $898 million.

However, if we were to include visitors to Singapore, the data is gloomy.

International visitor arrivals to Singapore in November 2019 was up 8.9% versus November 2018 to 1.53 million. The number of visitors from China grew 12.9% y-o-y to about 249,000 (i.e. 16.3% of all visitor arrivals are from China).

The growth in foreign visitors, taken together with the decline in retail sales value and the increase in F&B sales, seem to indicate that visitors are spending less, and when they do spend, they would rather spend on food than on shopping.

I made my rounds to about 10 malls on Saturday afternoon, 01 February 2020.

Although it was the 8th day of the Chinese New Year and heading towards Valentine's Day, the incessant news reports and multiple government directives surrounding the Coronavirus outbreak seemed to have kept most shoppers away from malls.

Sparse Orchard

The crowds at heartland malls seemed smaller than the usual crowd that I would expect during non-festive months. The traffic at both Orchard and Somerset MRT stations were weak for a Saturday afternoon.

The crowd size in several malls along Orchard Road seemed to be at or around the levels expected during a non-festive period.

And the number of shoppers carrying shopping bags was obviously limited.

With the Coronavirus outbreak still spreading and dominating the news, the contribution of foreign visitors' spend and the Chinese visitors' consumption and shopping, will surely be down for the next few months.

Adding to the woes of retailers in 2019, Honestbee, a retailer in liquidation, has offered 3 cents to the dollar to its creditors, with the rest of the debt converted to shares.

No matter how much we boast about per capita GDP, rising wages or stellar growth of household income, such is the state of retailers and e-commerce players in a tiny consumer market like Singapore's.

What is a jewel but something that just sparkles?

Looking further into the URA report, we note that 5.05 million sqft of lettable retail space was vacant (i.e. 7.5% vacancy rate) in 4Q19. This is equivalent to the lettable space of around five times that of VivoCity. The URA data about the increased prices and rentals of retail space in 2019 seem to be at odds with the amount of vacant shops and declining financial performance of retailers across the island.

I am hard-pressed to think if there might be an end to the plight of retail, particularly as some of the small strata-titled malls are being heralded as "ghost malls" by casual observers.

What surprised me most, buried in the URA 4Q19 numbers, is a new entry under "Uncompleted Commercial Projects with Approvals for Development" which shows that Changi Airport Group (S) Pte Ltd has obtained Planning Permission in November 2019 for a mixed development with 622,000 sqft of retail space!

Some might say that this will be another gem in Changi's crown. But some might ask, are we hastening the transfer of Singapore's sickly retail sector from ICU straight into the coffin?

18. Opportunities in Commercial and Industrial Markets for SMEs

First published in The Business Times, 19 December 2017

GDP growth has been revised upwards. Data for total trade and manufacturing output has been growing year-on-year since 2017 began. With most analysts claiming that the property sector will rebound in 2017 or 2018, every media story about the real estate sector is bullish.

Oddly, while property industry players are celebrating, the vacancies of office, retail, factory and warehouse space are setting new highs.

Data for third quarter 2017 shows that the vacancies of office, retail, factory and warehouse spaces, at 13.3 per cent, 8.2 per cent, 11.1 per cent and 12.5 per cent respectively, have well exceeded the vacancies experienced during the Global Financial Crisis in 2009. The 11.1 per cent vacancy in the factory segment translates to 45 million sqft of vacant production area.

Not surprisingly, monthly rentals and transacted prices of retail, factory and warehouse spaces dropped. However, data from the office sector went against logic: despite the total stock of vacant office space increasing by 872,000 sqft between June 30, 2017, and September 30, 2017, the rental and price indices increased by 2.4 per cent and 0.4 per cent respectively.

According to the Ministry of Manpower, total employment excluding foreign domestic workers contracted in the first nine months of 2017, with a total of 19,800 jobs lost.

The fundamental changes in the economy is causing us to experience healthy economic growth in manufacturing, services and trade, brought about by fewer people in the workforce with higher productivity and output.

This is one reason for the increasing stock of vacant space: we do not need the same amount of space to produce the same economic output. Another reason for the swathes of vacancies: a generous supply of space in new commercial clusters, business parks, innovation districts, regional centres, etc.

Given such mixed data, what should business owners do?

If you are a tenant of a commercial or industrial space, you can take heart that new supply coming on 2018-2020 will add further pressure to rentals. High vacancies also imply that tenants have a range of choices to consider for relocation. In short, we recommend business owners to seize this opportunity and plan for their business needs:

- Review your current space usage and the medium to long term growth plans of your business
- Decide on which spaces to reduce, where to expand or consolidate
- Negotiate for leases that are flexible, including contraction rights and sub-letting rights

Business owners could also consult with their trusted property advisers to map out a plan to take advantage of the current market weakness.

Reassess your needs

What if you owned the business premises? We can look at it in two ways.

If you are using the property for your business operations, you can consider if the property will still be relevant for your business over the medium to long term, say over the next 10 years.

You can reassess your needs and given the fast evolving global business environment, you might consider making your business more nimble-footed by doing a "sale-and-lease-back" of your commercial and industrial properties.

If you are a landlord and you invested in strata-titled commercial and industrial properties for rental income, you might want to consider if the product attributes such as location, size, layout and design are well-suited for long term holding as investments. Furthermore, note the length of the remaining leases of industrial properties.

The shorter leases of industrial properties, especially those with 30-year or 60-year leases, pose significant challenges during divestment as the prospective buyers of these properties often find difficulties in obtaining loans.

Singapore's economic fundamentals are shifting with technological disruptions. While we continue to be a magnet for new businesses coming into Asia, we are also seeing SMEs reduce their physical spaces in Singapore in order to pursue the plentiful opportunities overseas.

Given the rapid changes in manufacturing technology, 3D-printing and mass customisation, realignment of global logistics and supply chains and the new business trends involving e-contracts, blockchain and payment systems, business owners would do well to keep their businesses agile.

SMEs should consider taking advantage of the high vacancies in the commercial and industrial properties to re-group and plan their corporate real estate needs for the fast evolving economic landscape.

19. A Dark Cloud Looms Over Commercial Properties

With research support from Yeoh Theng and Aloysius Ng Shi Hao; first published on Storm-Asia.com, 20 May 2020

Remote working, flexible work arrangements and hot-desking have been discussed for over two decades, since the technological leaps of the dotcom boom era in the late 1990s. It was adopted, then stumbled, rehashed, sputtered. There was no coordinated will amongst multinational corporations (MNCs) to adopt flexible work arrangements.

Until COVID-19 came along and tilted the field. Or did it right the field by adjusting our mindset?

Many real estate analysts and operators and landlords of commercial spaces have repeatedly highlighted that demand for office space will remain strong. For example, due to distancing requirements and prior to having a vaccine, a company trying to accommodate the same number of workers would require possibly 20-50% more space.

Some employers are concerned that remote working does not help in building a shared company culture. Companies may have invested in expensive buildings or office renovations and would loath to see these investments wasted if a large percentage of their workers do not work from the office.

Then again, workers may not warm to the idea of being cooped up in their apartments, and if they have young children, they may not be productive at home.

For all these reasons, supporters of commercial real estate already conclude that there will be no decline in the take up of office space, and are already cheering for a post-COVID-19 recovery in real estate prices.

The changes we have seen

However, an article by MarketWatch published on 15 May 2020 suggested that a large number of tech employees in the USA will not want to return to their offices after COVID-19 is over.[1]

Recently, Twitter Inc. said its employees have the option of never coming back to the office to work, while Facebook Inc., Google parent Alphabet Inc., Salesforce.com Inc. and Slack Technologies Inc. have said they don't expect workers back in the office until 2021.

The article also quoted tech giant Cisco CEO Chuck Robbins: "Some elements of this work-from-home scenario will not go away."

The convenience and flexibility afforded by technology for video meetings such as Zoom, WebEx, Meet and Teams, or work collaboration tools such as Dropbox, Trello and Lark have been around for several years. COVID-19 forced us not only to incorporate these tools at work but to make regular use of them in the past few months.

---

1 Jon Swartz, "Work-from-home productivity pickup has tech CEOs predicting many employees will never come back to the office", *MarketWatch*, 30 May 2020, https://www.marketwatch.com/story/work-from-home-productivity-gain-has-tech-ceos-predicting-many-workers-will-never-come-back-to-the-office-2020-05-15

This Work From Home (WFH) phenomenon swept around the world at the same time. Business people were forced to interact with suppliers and customers remotely. Now, four months into the COVID-19 pandemic, many lawyers, bankers and professionals have adapted to online business activities such as the signing of multi-million-dollar contracts, banking transactions, court hearings, funds management, corporate accounting, etc.

The result will be that many business professionals now realise they are more productive working remotely. They complete tasks faster and more efficiently without having to be physically in their offices and they save commuting time and expenses. The companies they work for could economise on future rental budgets.

We foresee that many employees will opt to work from home on a more permanent basis, or work anywhere else outside of their offices say, in a park, a library or a cafe.

This bottom-up demand from employees allows MNCs to study their office space needs for the next 5 to 10 years.

The advantages do not end there

Companies able to increase the proportion of staff on flexible work arrangements may face less business disruptions and have better business continuity should another disease outbreak or natural disaster happen.

Sales people can multiply the number of sales calls they can make every week as travel is reduced, especially with overseas clients.

MNCs can hire top talent from abroad without the talent having to leave their hometown. For example, a Singapore pharmaceutical company may hire a researcher from Thailand on its Singapore payroll and adopt a remote work arrangement, avoiding applications

Fig. 1: Summary of Office Space in Singapore

1st Quarter 2020	
Available office floor space (Nett Lettable Area)	87.6 million sqft
Occupied office floor space (Nett Lettable Area)	78.0 million sqft
Vacant office floor space (Nett Lettable Area)	9.6 million sqft
Vacancy rate	11.0%
Upcoming supply (Gross Floor Area)	7.8 million sqft

Source: Urban Redevelopment Authority and International Property Advisor

for an Employment Pass in Singapore. The researcher will be paid a Singapore salary but does not require an expatriate's housing and travel package.

Not all companies will have 100% of their staff work remotely. But given the global recession, 100% of companies will rethink their corporate real estate strategy, reducing employee time in the office through staggering work days or hours.

The impact of these changes will lead to a nett reduction of demand for space.

Office space in Singapore

The vacancy of office space hovered around 11% for the past three years.

In 1Q2020, just prior to the impact of COVID-19, some 9.6 million sqft of office space laid vacant across Singapore. This is equivalent to having more than nine Vivocity blocks of office space sitting vacant. The high volume of vacant space reflected anaemic business demand, increasing efficiency of space utilisation through co-working arrangements as well as a consistent supply of new office space.

An additional 7.8 million sqft of office space is planned for, or under construction.

Even prior to any significant impact of COVID-19, some 19,000 businesses and companies ceased operations in the first three months of 2020.[2]

After COVID-19 hit Singapore, 8,663 companies ceased operations just in April.[3]

As government support schemes expire in the second half of this year, we expect more businesses to close and more office workers to be laid off.

Of particular concern are tourism, transport and travel related businesses, most of which might never recover from this downturn. And pains in the oil and gas sector have just begun to show.

COVID-19 will change workers' and organisations' behaviours, and it will reduce the demand for offices. Added to that are businesses failing or downsizing during this pandemic-led recession.

If we take a modest drop of 10% of the current office usage, that would result in occupied office space dropping from 78 million sqft to about 70 million sqft. Vacant space would then increase to almost 18 million sqft or 20%.

---

2 Joyce Lim, "Coronavirus pandemic deals fatal blow to struggling businesses", *The Straits Times*, 6 April 2020, https://www.straitstimes.com/business/economy/pandemic-deals-fatal-blow-to-struggling-businesses

3 Tay Peck Gek, "Over 8,500 business entities close shop in April; highest in recent years", *The Business Times*, 11 May 2020, https://www.sgsme.sg/news/over-8500-business-entities-close-shop-april-highest-recent-years

Perhaps real estate consultant CBRE's forecast for Grade A office rents to drop by 13.0% in 2020 and then rebound 4.5% in 2021[4] is a tad optimistic.

While it is too early to make any definitive statements about the extent that COVID-19 will alter the economy, we can be sure that landlords will need to up their game and offer a lot more incentives to keep office space occupied.

4 Cecillia Chow, "CBRE's Moray Armstrong sees 'a raft of opportunities' post-Covid-19", EdgeProp, 15 May 2020, https://www.edgeprop.sg/property-news/cbre's-moray-arm-strong-sees-'-raft-opportunities'-post-covid-19

PART 5

OTHERS - INVESTING OVERSEAS, DEBUNKING MYTHS & WEALTH TRANSFER

20. Do Your Homework When Venturing Overseas

Co-authored with Desmond Tay; first published in The Business Times,
13 September 2018

For those investing for inter-generational wealth transfer, the abundance of overseas properties with freehold tenure is a big draw. The spread of overseas property investment options is staggering.

Locations range from Sydney to London to New York and many cities in between. The array of property types include the familiar segments such as residential, office and retail shops, and the somewhat exotic segments such as farms, hotel rooms, carpark lots, hostels, aged care facilities and real estate debt.

Spoilt by the multitude of choices across the world, how does an investor tell what are genuinely good investments?

A recent article on Bloomberg titled *The End of the Global Housing Boom* stated that house prices in major capital cities are heading south, caused by increasing taxes to reduce demand, tighter borrowing rules and home values being out of whack with affordability.

The article highlighted the weakening demand and declining prices in London, Sydney, Beijing and New York and forewarned of the risks of contagion effects: rich investors have enjoyed low interest rates buying homes across multiple cities; once these investors are forced to realise their losses in one city, they might have to sell out in other cities too.

The article is correct, particularly in the segment of luxury homes where the wealthy are buying homes to rent to the wealthy, rental demand simply falls short of supply! For most of the markets that we keep track of, luxury residences are over-supplied while mass affordable housing is sorely insufficient.

This is particularly true for most of the countries in Southeast Asia, perhaps with the exception of Singapore. Investors who are purely focused on the residential segment could do well to search for opportunities in mass affordable housing in countries such as Malaysia, Indonesia, Cambodia, Thailand and Vietnam.

By mass affordable housing, we are referring to homes that are priced at about three to five years of a factory production worker's household income.

Beyond Southeast Asia, we observe the following trends with regard to the popular markets of Australia and the UK, and more recently, Japan. Here is a summary of a few key markets which we track and our recommendations.

Country	What is interesting?	Recommendation
Southeast Asia	Large populations ascending from the lower to the middle class, coupled with steady increases in household incomes and relatively youthful demographics will drive demand for affordable housing. A new government in Malaysia, and potentially new governments in Indonesia and Thailand may bring better economic prospects and improved real estate values.	Invest in mass affordable housing where the shortage is unlikely to be filled within the next decade. Stay clear of the luxury segment unless employment laws are favourable for large numbers of expatriate families to move in. Take note that currency controls and fluctuations, together with withholding taxes could dampen investment returns significantly.

Country	What is interesting?	Recommendation
England	Terms of Brexit are still cloudy and the exodus of EU and foreign nationals from the UK will exceed the number of British nationals returning to the UK. The reduction of EU education grants is expected to draw a majority of EU students back home to enjoy free university education instead of having to pay foreign students' fees in UK universities.	Avoid investing in England's real estate until the dust has settled a year or two after Brexit is completed. This also goes for student hostels especially those outside London.
Australia	Tight loan rules and increased taxes have weakened foreign demand. Installing the sixth prime minister in eight years at the end of August 2018 also added downward pressure on the real estate market. However, Australia powers the world with its energy and mineral resources and feeds the world with its agricultural products so the long-term outlook remains positive.	Stay on the sidelines and watch for a resurgence in global demand for commodities before investing. For those who are long Australian dollars and need to invest immediately, and given that developers are hard-pressed for financing, do consider financing developers' debt – an avenue open to retail investors. Take note that the resale market for Australian homes is small, as second-hand homes can be resold only to Australian nationals and permanent residents.
Japan	After two lost decades, the property market woke up over the past six years when Prime Minister Shinzo Abe deregulated industries and opened doors by relaxing visa restrictions to welcome foreign students, foreign workers and tourists. Thirty universities conduct degree and postgraduate programmes in English with fees from around S$7,000 per year. There are close to a million jobs waiting to be filled. No surprises that the number of foreign students and foreigners residing in Japan is breaking record highs every year for the past six years. A residential apartment in the popular Tokyo districts of Shinjuku and Shibuya will rent for 4-6 per cent gross yield. It is rare to find property titles that are not freehold.	Demand for real estate, particularly residences in the major cities, should be sustained for the next decade or so. The expected decline in population is not happening as much as predicted due to the influx of foreign skilled workers. Take note that Japan's property transactions and both sellers and buyers need to pay up to 3 per cent fees to the agents representing them.

Do your homework

I sound like a broken record when I remind investors and fellow property agents to consider the risks and potential stumbling blocks around investing in properties overseas. The first pitfall that plagues most investors is not having done sufficient homework to research the foreign markets.

On the other hand, I have also seen investors who have done too much homework and missed the 30 per cent total returns (capital appreciation and rental income) they would have gained from Japan's property market in the past four years. Furthermore, many investors rely purely on new foreign properties launched in Singapore without considering that completed properties with tenants might give better returns.

Investors should also consider the post-investment activities such as: how would you secure your first tenant, who will collect the monthly rentals on your behalf, is there a trustworthy agent who will manage the property, how do you report and pay taxes in the foreign country, who will help you sell the property when you need to divest, what is the estimated total returns after divestment and remitting the money back to Singapore?

Higher returns for higher risks

Regardless of asset classes, investors are exposed to significantly more risks when investing overseas as compared with investing in Singapore. Given the higher risks, investors must demand higher returns that will offset the risks, and cover the additional effort required.

No matter how beautiful the scenery at that skilodge or how enjoyable that beach resort experience was, properties that do not provide higher returns over and above the increased risks and effort should be avoided. Invest with your heads, not with your hearts.

Case Study: A Curious Case of "No Money Down" Property Schemes

Co-authored with Joel Kam; first published on PropertySoul.com, 15 May 2019

We present the case of John and his parents. John is an undergraduate who has taken finance and investment classes that cover a range of asset-types, including real estate. During a family dinner, when discussing a module that John was taking in the university, Real Estate Investments and Finance, his parents divulged that they made a real estate investment several years ago: a 3-bedroom freehold condominium unit in Johor, Malaysia.

Their decision to commit was based on 3 key factors:

1. They believe that real estate is a safe asset that will constantly grow in value. If held for long enough, the capital gains will return a hefty sum. Surely, real estate is a worthwhile investment with little downside risk.
2. They trusted their friend's 'hot tip' and dived head-first without weighing all the costs and benefits that the investment might bring. They assumed that if it was a good investment for their close friend, it was good for them too.
3. Best of all, they loved the NO MONEY DOWN proposition! The property sold by the developer came with 100% financing from a

bank in Malaysia! Other than RM$5,000 administration fee and legal costs, they did not have to pay down the mortgage until the property was completed and rentals started rolling in.

They thought: why not own another property in addition to the one in Singapore? Things could not get any better than this. The property has a freehold title and is located in a middle-high end residential neighbourhood with a mall complete with all the necessary amenities: schools, nurseries, clinics, etc., within half an hour's drive to Singapore.

Four years later, around mid-2018, the property was completed. The 15-year mortgage kicked-in on the RM$618,800 principal at 4.5% p.a. interest. They were repaying RM$5,000 a month to the bank.

During the 10 months, there were no calls looking to rent the apartment.

So it has been purely cash outflow, with maintenance expenses, property tax, utilities bills and of course the hefty mortgage.

This NO MONEY DOWN deal in Johor made matters worse for the family's finances.

John's parents have taken on three corporate loans for their family business. Liabilities due in the next two years amount to about S$380,000, i.e. regular payments of about S$16,000 each month. Amidst the slow business environment for engineering contractors in Singapore, their monthly cash flow for the business and family struggled to stay positive.

So how did their 'brilliant' investment opportunity fare to date? The initial price of the 3-bedroom apartment of 1,097 sqft was RM$618,800. A quick online survey of various property websites resulted in a few dozen listings which indicated an asking price range of RM$308,000-700,000. Half of the listings for similar-sized 3-bedroom units were below RM$440,000, with the lowest being RM$308,000 which was amongst a handful that were listed under "foreclosure sales". There was a single listing at RM$700,000, a clear outlier as the next highest listing we could find was at RM$598,000.

Price Category (MYR)	Number of listings
300,000 – 399,999	13
400,000 – 499,999	3
500,000 – 599,999	8
600,000 – 699,999	0
700,000 – 799,999	1

Source: iproperty.com.my

Taking the top outlier out of the picture, the average market price of the two dozen listings was around RM$430,000. For John's parents, assuming that they are able to divest the apartment at RM$430,000, they will suffer a capital loss of RM$188,800, or about 30%, over the past five years, excluding other costs.

This is a massive loss for a family which has barely enough money to tide through daily living expenses.

This capital loss will be further exacerbated by the fact that they have signed up a 100% Loan-to-Value (LTV) mortgage for the RM$618,800 investment. This loan has a fixed interest rate of 4.5% per annum. Over the 15-year loan tenure, the interest will cost about RM$230,000. Adding that to the principal sum, John's parents would need to foot a massive RM$850,000 over the 15-year period.

Alternatively, if John's parents decide to sell the property at the average market price today, they would still need to foot a loss of

RM$188,800 plus interest expenses and legal costs. Since "no money" was put up at the start, even a slight decrease in value from the original amount of the property would give us a negative return on investment. What a way to beat the market.

Assuming that today's market is indeed at RM$430,000, should John wait for the market to pick up, he would have to wait for Malaysia's real estate market to rebound by 10% a year continuously for the next five years before he can break even on the investment. However, there do not seem to be many interested buyers at this price, which is why foreclosure sales are priced from a mere RM$308,000. If John had to divest at RM$308,000, the capital loss will be RM$310,800 before fees and expenses.

So, what went wrong? A deeper reflection on the entire picture will show us just how many and how deep the caveats are in such an 'investment strategy', as well as the lessons John learnt from this case.

1. If it's too good to be true, then it probably is

We hope that the age-old saying is not true. We always hope for a better life for our family. That hope makes us feel as if we have to outperform the market to get 'out of the rat race' and head towards 'financial freedom'. But get-rich-quick schemes are never the solution. These are schemes that tap on our insecurities in the hope that we ignore all the 'what-ifs' that could get us into more financial troubles. 'No money down' property schemes are highly risky investments with too many what-ifs for investors. Even for highly experienced real estate investors such as REITs managers, the rules limit their gearing ratio to a maximum of 45%.

2. Pick up a book (or go to your best friend, Google)

A major reason why many fall prey to such schemes or scams is due to the lack of research about the asset class they are investing in

Basing your research on a 'gut feeling' which many claim as their 'keen acumen', or a 'hot tip' from a friend or relative is obviously insufficient. Any investment of any kind requires good solid research to back up, both quantitative and qualitative. If you're not sure, pay a trustworthy expert to do the due diligence for you. Read a book related to the asset class or simply google it! And do make sure that you check on the reliability of the sources too.

3. If at first you don't succeed... err... try something else

It does not always have to be real estate. Good investments can be found in many areas around us. Invest in something you understand. If you can't understand the asset class well enough, chances are it's not a well-suited investment for you. Real estate as an asset class requires more than just betting that the market will go up or down in your favour. There is one revenue line and many lines of cost components involved in generating the overall returns that have to be considered. If that sounds too foreign for you, try investing in an asset class that's a lot more understandable.

It would be foolish for one to think that he knows how to invest in real estate simply because he has lived in real estate his whole life.

Question: If you were caught in a similar situation, what might be your next steps be?

22. Real Estate Versus Inflation: A Problematic Narrative

In Singapore's real estate market, one of the longest surviving old wives' tales must be "real estate is a hedge against inflation".

When we were younger, playgrounds dates were a thing and dating meant finding the courage to ask someone out in person, face-to-face. Yes, and policemen wore bermudas then. Most of that has changed, a lot. Teenagers now busy themselves with gadgets while computer games and dating apps have changed the entire scene altogether. As we progress, we accept new concepts and adopt new ways of doing things.

Yet for some reason, we remain stuck with a folklore that seems immovable.

Investment blogs such as Dollars&Sense,[1] news commentaries[2] and academic literature[3] also perpetuate this folklore.

1 Dinesh Dayani, "4 Investments That Naturally Hedges Against Inflation In Singapore", *Dollars and Sense*, 27 February 2018, https://dollarsandsense.sg/4-investments-naturally-hedges-inflation-singapore/
2 Sing Tien Foo and Chia Liu Ee, "Commentary: Did aggressive land bidding by Chinese developers push up Singapore property prices?", *ChannelNewsAsia*, 11 August 2019, https://www.channelnewsasia.com/news/commentary/land-bidding-chinese-developers-singapore-property-rising-cost-11764932
3 Dalina Amonhaemanon, Marc J.K.De Ceuster, Jan Annaert and Hau Le Long, "The Inflation-hedging Ability of Real Estate Evidence in Thailand: 1987-2011", Procedia Economics and Finance, Volume 5, 2013, Pages 40-49, https://www.sciencedirect.com/science/article/pii/S2212567113000075; Tien-Foo National and Swee-Hiang Low, "The Inflation-Hedging Characteristics of Real Estate and Financial Assets in Singapore", Journal of Real Estate Portfolio Management, 18 June 2020, https://www.tandfonline.com/doi/abs/10.1080/10835547.2000.12089623"

Accommodation costs account for nearly 23% in the basket of goods used for calculating Singapore's Consumer Price Index (CPI). The CPI – All Items index is one measure of inflation and I urge readers to familiarize themselves with the basket of goods and their various weights in the CPI by reading the educational material on this topic provided on the Department of Statistics' website.[4] Other major components of the CPI include Food (21.7%), Healthcare (6.2%), Private Transport (15.8%) and Education (6.2%).

To tabulate the costs of accommodation, statisticians track residential <u>rental</u> data. Accommodation can be split into both rentals and owner-occupied homes. About 90% of Singapore Citizen and Permanent Resident (collectively known as "Singapore Resident") households live in owner-occupied homes. The cost of housing for this owner-occupier group is not directly observed for, unlike those who live in rented homes. As a result, the cost of accommodation for the owner-occupier group is proxied using rentals instead. However, the people who generate demand for rented homes are, by far and large, NOT Singaporeans.

Of the 10% of Singapore resident households that live in rented homes, the low-income households that rent the roughly 60,000 small-sized HDB flats form the majority.

As a result, the "Accommodation" component of the CPI is mainly contributed by foreigners renting homes in this country. And if their demand for rental homes goes up or goes down, and it moves the CPI, does it directly impact Singapore resident households who are living in owner-occupied homes?

So what are the origins of the folklore? How much truth is in the underlying message? Is the statement still relevant in this day and age?

---

4 "Singapore Consumer Price Index (CPI)", *Department of Statistics Singapore*, https://www.Singstat.gov.sg/modules/infographics/consumer-price-index

In this article, we present some of the reasons why this message is no longer relevant and why we think it should stop being propagated.

First off, what is inflation?

"Inflation" refers to a general increase in prices of consumer goods and services, which leads to a fall in the purchasing value of money. Simply put, inflation is the reason our Hokkien noodles and kopi-O lunch cost $3.80 ten years ago, but cost $5.00 today. The price increased due to demand factors from consumers, and cost factors from ingredients, wages, rent and equipment, or a combination of both higher demand and input costs.

Should demand for consumer goods and services rise faster than supply, inflation would occur. Similarly, if costs of input items of goods, labour, overheads, compliance, rent and services rise, vendors would be forced to increase prices to stay afloat. Hence inflation.

Real estate has its own demand and supply factors which need to be considered. Within the real estate sector are different segments, for example: residential, office, retail, hotels and industrial. Each segment has its unique drivers for demand and supply.

For residential properties, the primary demand comes from people who need a place to live in. They could purchase their own home. Or they could pay rent to those who purchased a dwelling unit as an investment. The point is subtle and I wish readers to take note: the primary demand for a residential property comes from someone who needs to live in the property. That primary demand may be satisfied by someone buying a residential property for his own use or by renting the property from someone who had purchased it as an investment. A property that is purchased while it is still under construction does not satisfy the primary demand for housing. It satisfied the primary demand for investment.

On the other hand, the supply or availability of residential properties may be measured by how many housing units are available for rent and actively looking for tenants. It could also be measured by the number of residential units available for sale by property developers (this source is considered the primary supply market), as well as the number of units available for sale from owners who are not developers (i.e. the secondary market).

Many external factors can cause increases or decreases in both demand and supply, and therefore affect property prices and rents. For example, an economic crisis could cause investors to postpone their purchases, therefore decreasing demand and widening the demand-supply gap. Housing prices are pressured downwards when the demand for housing falls more than supply. The same economic crisis will also lead to lower incomes such that tenants will negotiate for lower rents. The converse is true: prices and rents will increase if demand exceeds supply, or if supply falls off while demand remains.

However, inflation can remain positive during an economic crisis. In fact, in many developing countries, economic downturns usually depress the exchange rates of the countries which leads to increased inflation as the costs of imported ingredients jump. During such periods, inflation continues to rise while tenants seek lower rentals such that inflation and rents go in opposite directions. Which means that as the owner of the property, you will be collecting lower and lower rents while dealing with higher costs, such as during the period from late 2013 to late 2017 (see Fig. 1). Due to the oversupply of residential units and declining rentals, owning a private residential property is hardly a hedge against inflation.

Fig. 1: Graph showing the increase in MAS Core Inflation index and Private Property Rental index from Q1 1993 to Q2 2020 [data before 1Q1993 not available]. Shaded areas indicate the periods where rentals were dropping while inflation continued to trend up.

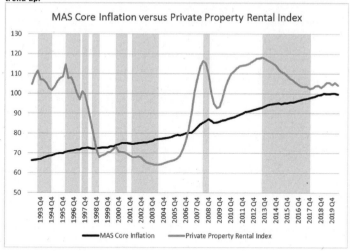

Source: Singstat, International Property Advisor

Fig. 2 and 3: Prices of resale HDB flats and private properties moved contrary to inflation about a third of the time during the last 28 years.

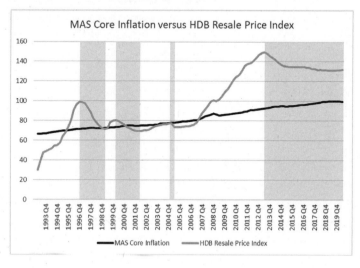

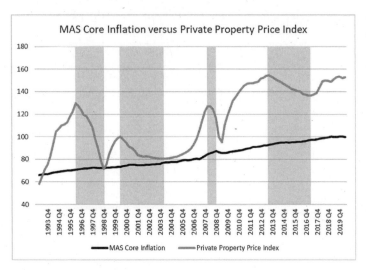

Source: Singstat, International Property Advisor

Learning point 1:

For real estate to be considered a hedge against inflation, home prices and rentals would need to increase at minimally the same rate as inflation or better still, exceed the pace of inflation altogether. From the figures above, we see that at various points in the last three decades, housing costs moved against inflation. So to say that owning a home will allow one to hedge the effects of inflation, it depends on when one buys and sells the home. And for the 95% of us in Singapore who live in 99-year-lease HDB flats and private housing, we have not even considered the effect of depreciating leases on home values. Are we over-generalizing when we say that home ownership will shield us from inflation?

The old wives' tale is irrelevant going forward

Many of us would look at Fig. 1 to 3 and still be tempted to conclude that the adage is true over the 28-year period. Afterall, with the exception of the private residential rental index (Fig. 1), the HDB Resale Price index (Fig. 2) and Private Property Price index (Fig. 3) increased by more than core inflation during the same period.

But that method of thinking presents a logical fallacy by itself. It fails to consider that many other factors come into play. To determine what the trend will be like, we need to first ask ourselves the following questions:

1. Will the components that drive inflation in the past be the same as those that drive inflation in the next 10 to 20 years?
2. Assuming that core inflation continues on a positive 1% growth indefinitely in the future, will housing prices increase indefinitely too?

Inflation levels are "managed" under the watchful eyes of the Monetary Authority of Singapore (MAS) and they maintain a foreign exchange policy that prioritises price stability for consumer goods in Singapore. Singapore has a small consumer base and our cost of living depends largely on imported goods. By varying exchange rates, MAS is able to maintain price stability, with a slight uptrend (i.e. inflation) for consumers. The slight uptrend means a depreciation of the value of money as the same S$1 tomorrow will buy less goods and services than the S$1 today.

Why the MAS needs to maintain inflation as a positive number, rather than maintaining it at 0% is anyone's guess. I am not an economist and I do not buy the theory that a small positive inflation is better than zero inflation.

What I would like to determine is whether housing prices will increase at the same or higher rate than inflation in the future. While it has done so historically, there is no causal link which can explain the relationship between inflation and the increase in housing prices. Correlation between the two variables does not equal to causation. When one looks at data, it is not sufficient to use historical data to extrapolate possible future trends. Statistical evidence should be used hand-in-hand with logical and contextual evidence to produce a more convincing analysis.

To illustrate this, we compared the core inflation index to that of the price indexes of some other categories of goods below.

Fig. 4: MAS Core Inflation index versus selected component indices of inflation

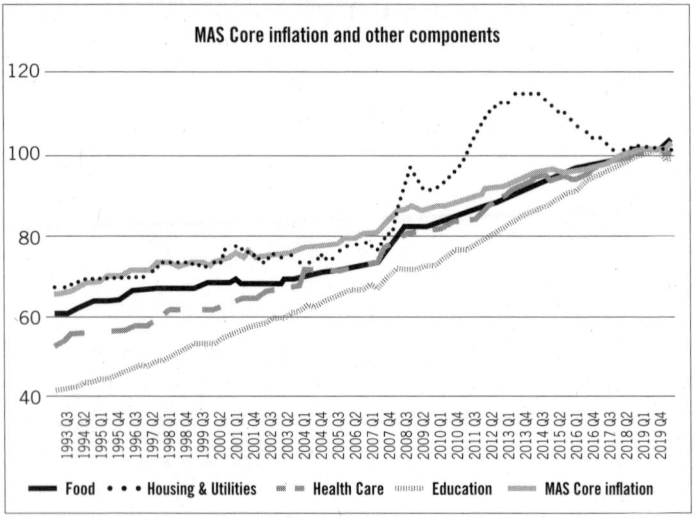

Source: Singstat, International Property Advisor

We can see from Fig. 4 that the other components such as Food, Housing & Utilities (which accounts for rental and utility prices), Health Care and Education all increase along with MAS Core Inflation. With the exception of Housing & Utilities (which increased 30 index points over the 28 years as compared to inflation which increased 35 points), all the other components also rose with a steeper increase than the Core Inflation index.

Based on the graph above, investments in any of the components could be used as "inflation hedges". Yet, none of us have been advised to invest in the businesses of Food, or Education, or Health Care in order to beat inflation.

The most common justification for this old wives' tale is the argument that as wages increase, inflation will increase as well. An increase in wages would mean that tenants can afford to, and are willing to, pay higher rentals, and hence market rentals are pushed up. But this argument is weak: just because wages increase does not mean people will pay higher rentals, especially if the supply of homes is much greater than demand due to over-construction, or in the past few years, decline in foreigner demand. Put it in another way: if this were true, given that median household incomes have increased about 20% in the last five years, food at hawker centres would have gone from $5 to $6.

One might also refer to the different sub-periods in the figures above to argue that real estate could be a good hedge during some periods. That argument however remains flawed due to two reasons:

1. It is easy to use historical data to conclude that a particular sub-period might have been best. Unless the cause-effect relationship is direct, we should not use historical data to predict the future.

2. Within these sub-periods (e.g. Lehman Crisis), the valuations of most asset classes, including shares, commodities, art, etc, dropped. One could invest in any of these assets, not just real estate, as they provide 'strong inflation hedges' when the economy turns positive and valuations go up.

The question then is why should we choose real estate as a hedge against inflation? Of the 10 broad categories (known as "divisions") of consumer expenses in Fig. 5, which of the items will grow in weight and importance as Singapore's population ages in future? Should we not be investing in the categories such as Health Care and Food to hedge against their rising costs?

Fig. 5: Table of components that make up the Consumer Price Index

DEPARTMENT OF
STATISTICS
SINGAPORE

SINGAPORE CONSUMER PRICE INDEX (2014 = 100)
JANUARY 2019

TABLE 1
CONSUMER PRICE INDEX
(2014 = 100)

Division	Weights (%)	% Change Jan 2019 / Jan 2018	% Change Jan 2019 / Dec 2018
ALL ITEMS	100.0	0.4	-0.3
Food	21.7	1.4	0.3
Clothing & Footwear	2.7	2.5	0.8
Housing & Utilities	26.3	-0.5	-1.8
Household Durables & Services	4.7	0.7	-0.1
Health Care	6.1	1.7	0.5
Transport	15.8	-1.8	0.3
Communication	3.9	-2.9	0.0
Recreation & Culture	7.9	0.9	-1.8
Education	6.1	3.2	1.3
Miscellaneous Goods & Services	4.8	1.4	0.6
All Items less Imputed Rentals on Owner-Occupied Accommodation[1]	81.0	0.9	-0.3
All Items less Accommodation	77.1	1.0	0.1
MAS Core Inflation Measure	65.6	1.7	0.1

[1] A significant share of the CPI Accommodation group is "owner-occupied accommodation (OOA) cost", which is computed based on the imputed rental concept under the rental equivalence method. Besides the imputed rentals on OOA, actual rentals paid on rented units are included separately under the CPI Accommodation group. Given that imputed rentals on OOA have no impact on the cash expenditure of most households in Singapore as they already own their homes, "All Items less imputed rentals on OOA" is compiled as an additional indicator.

Source: Singstat

Learning point 2:

Consumer inflation is affected by the prices of a basket of many different items. Investing in commodities, energy, food, transport, healthcare or the shares of companies related to these businesses might allow one to hedge against inflation.

Looking to the academics for pointers

If this old wives' tale were true, surely the finance, economics and real estate professors must have researched it extensively and published various papers in top journals to nail down this claim?

Our search returned with disappointing results. Published literature is scant and are mainly focused on the use of real estate shares (i.e. developers and REITs listed on stock exchanges) as a possible inflation hedge. Even here, the evidence is mixed. There is hardly any literature on the use of physical real estate as a hedge against inflation. The studies that include physical real estate are normally confined to commercial real estate, rather than residential ones, as our well-meaning friends and relatives might have encouraged us to do.

Commercial real estate makes more sense as an inflation hedge since economic expansion naturally pushes corporate rentals, and inflation, up. It will not be correct however, to say that the relationship would continue to hold especially as more businesses see less of a need for a physical retail space amidst the growing adoption of e-commerce or physical office space given the wider adoption of remote working. Home-based businesses may also price goods more competitively due to the absence of rentals for physical shop spaces, reducing the impact on inflationary pressures.

Academic research on this subject are few and far between. We must also be aware of the geographical differences in which these studies are carried out. For example, Japan's real estate environment is different from USA's, Europe's and Singapore's. While a study conducted in one country might show that real estate is a possible hedge for inflation, that relationship might not hold into perpetuity, nor apply to Singapore.

On this subject and specific to Singapore, we found one paper. In "The Inflation-Hedging characteristics of Real Estate and Financial Assets in Singapore" (Sing and Low, 2000)[5] the authors suggest that while real estate (as a whole) provides a better hedge against inflation than stocks and securitized real estate investments, the

---

5 https://www.tandfonline.com/doi/abs/10.1080/10835547.2000.12089623

inflation-hedging ability of residential properties is only effective when hedging against *unexpected inflation in a low inflation* regime.

This is rather curious since low inflation regime environments are the periods of time in which we should be least worried about inflation or hedging against it. And how would one hedge against inflation that is "unexpected"?

In fact, the paper concluded that amongst the four segments of real estate, i.e. office, shop, industrial and residential, only **industrial** properties offer a strong hedge for both expected and unexpected inflation during periods of high inflation while **shop** offers significant hedge only against expected inflation.

This research paper published in 2000 based on reviews of historical data from 1978 to 1998 further confounds the issue why the old wives' tale survived two decades later such that Singaporeans continue to invest in residential properties as a 'safe bet'.

Learning point 3:
The amount of academic research supporting this old wives' tale for Singapore real estate is thin. The single research paper we found on Singapore looked back over two decades and the authors concluded that there was no evidence that owning residential properties could shield investors against inflation.

Looking into the future
We mentioned at the start of this article that certain events can occur which can catalyze changes in the demand or supply of real estate. Housing prices will be affected such that its relationship with inflation may be altered. Whilst disasters, crises and pandemics cannot be forecasted, we can look at certain immutable trends to understand what the future demand or supply numbers would look like.

One major trend to watch is the demographic changes in Singapore. This is especially relevant for residential property investment since the demand and supply of homes is dependent on the number of people renting, buying and selling them.

Fig. 6: Singapore's population pyramid in 2020

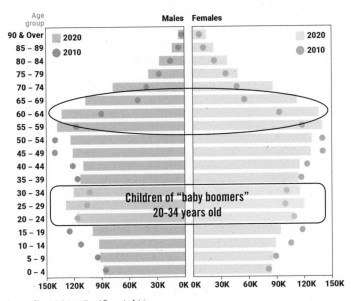

Source: Singstat, International Property Advisor

Let us look at Singapore's demographics using the population pyramid (Fig. 6). The cohorts of residents in the age bands of 55 to 69 represent the baby boomers who grew up during the nation building years. These are the ones sold on the rhetoric of the need for home ownership as a stable roof over their heads. Home ownership within this group is likely to be close to 100%.

The children of baby boomers, currently in the age bands of 20 to 34, have been actively buying properties in the last 10 years and about 200,000 new HDB flats and 100,000 new Executive Condominiums and private residences have been launched to satisfy their demand. The buying from this group will slow significantly in the next 10 years as most who could afford to buy would have bought.

The challenge will come over the next 20-25 years when the baby boomers pass on, downgrade, or move in with their kids for ease of elderly care. As our life expectancy at age 65 is another 21.3 years, we would expect to see many baby boomers passing away in the next 25 years when more than 500,000 of them would have crossed their 86th birthday. More than half would have passed on.

Upon the demise of the remaining partner, their children will divest their HDB flats in the resale market because most of the surviving children are already home owners and, by law, are unable to inherit the HDB flats.

As for the baby boomers who pass on their private residences, it would also be presumptuous to assume that their children would keep these private residences for 'investment purposes', especially since many of these properties would be aged and might require a lot of maintenance and renovations. The older 99-year properties would also be steadily decaying in value and it would be burdensome to hold on to such properties for rent. Children of baby boomers are more likely to sell these inherited properties and split the cash proceeds amongst the siblings and beneficiaries.

The divestment of these 'hand-me-down' properties will add to the number of residential properties in the HDB and private resale markets. This will then have the effect of pushing down prices of residential properties as the supply increases due to the passing of the baby boomers en masse.

Look further down the population tree to the age cohorts of infants to 14-year-olds and we can see that there will be insufficient numbers in these cohorts to purchase the thousands of resale properties and new launches (assuming new launches are not pared back significantly).

Therefore, unless Singapore is able to create massive numbers of jobs and welcome hundreds of thousands of foreigners as Permanent Residents and new citizens, the downside risks over the next 25 years for the residential market will largely outweigh the rosy property dreams painted by property agents, analysts and the older generation.

Rising property prices should not be extrapolated indefinitely, as oversupply risks pile on due to our ageing demographics. In the meantime, inflation will continue to rise, pushed up by rising health care demand and costs.

The average Singapore investor, whose wealth is mostly locked up in physical real estate, would be foolish to ignore the fact that everyone will eventually die and that we have a large population of baby boomers approaching their life expectancy of 86. Hopefully, this argument helps to dispel this gross overconfidence in the continual rise in residential property prices.

Learning point 4:
To hedge against inflationary pressures in the future years, investors should consider the irreversible trends of the ageing population and the resulting increase in resale properties.

The use of real estate for investment diversification

Does that mean that the old wives' tale has no basis?

Institutional or large investors do use real estate equities or physical real estate (though it is normally the former) as an asset class to hedge their portfolio risks and for risk diversification purposes. However, the context here is rather different than for individual investors.

To understand this, we first have to understand the basic principles and need for diversification in a portfolio. In finance textbooks and in the investment world, the primary reason investment managers want diversification is that they need to lower their risks of concentrating too much investment in a single asset class. This is an application of the adage 'don't put all your eggs in one basket'.

We can explain this using a simplified example. Assume that investor A has $100 million in cash to invest. If A were to invest all his money into the stocks of company XYZ, if anything were to go wrong with the company, he could potentially lose a large portion if not all of his stake. If he invested in various companies in the stock market, he could have reduced the probability of losing all $100 million by a large amount, especially if he invested across different sectors and geographies.

This diversification with stocks as an asset class however, is limited since the performance of the individual stocks is largely tied to the performance of the stock market as a whole. In times of economic boom, stocks generally increase in value at a much higher rate (i.e. bull market) than in an economic downturn (i.e. bear market).

That is where diversification of asset classes comes in handy. To choose the right asset class to use as a diversifier, we must first look at the historical correlation between the assets we want to hedge against and the assets which we would like to use as a hedge.

Fig. 7: Correlation between asset classes.

	Global equities	Global bonds	Global listed real estate	Global direct real estate
Global equities	1.0	-0.8	0.7	0.4
Global bonds		1.0	-0.3	-0.1
Global listed real estate			1.0	0.6
Global direct real estate				1.0

Source: UBS Asset Management "Real Estate: Navigating your investment journey", Edition 2017

This table shows the correlation between four different asset classes and was taken from a UBS Asset Management report released in 2017. Read this correlation matrix starting from the right-most column "Global Direct Real Estate". It shows that Global Direct Real Estate has a correlation of 0.4, -0.1 and 0.6 respectively with Global Equities, Global Bonds and Global Listed Real Estate. Global Listed Real Estate refers to the asset class that is made up of the prices of shares of real estate developers and Real Estate Investment Trusts that are listed on stock exchanges around the world.

A positive correlation means that as the prices of Global Direct Real Estate move up, Global Equities prices will increase in price, and vice versa. A positive correlation of 1.0 means that a 1% increase in Global Direct Real Estate prices will see the other asset class increase by 1%. Correlations of 1.0 mean that the two assets move perfectly in tandem with one another. Negative correlation on the other hand means that as one asset class increases in price, the other falls in price. A perfect negative correlation of -1.0 means that a 1% increase in the first asset will see a 1% decrease in the price of the other asset.

Having imperfect correlations between a few asset classes allows a portfolio manager to diversify the investment portfolio and reduce concentration risks. The lower the correlations between asset classes, the better the diversification.

Assume that the $100 million portfolio is split equally: 50% in Global Equities and 50% in Global Direct Real Estate.

Based on the correlation of 0.4 between these two asset classes, a 10% decrease in the prices of Global Equities he owns, will only cause an average decrease of 4% in the Global Direct Real Estate value he owns. That will bring the overall portfolio value loss to 7% (50% x -10% + 50% x -4%), instead of the full loss of 10% had he held the entire portfolio in equities.

Of course, this method of diversification will not just limit losses during a downturn, but will also limit the total gains during a market uptick. However, for fund managers who are investing money on behalf of clients, defensive strategies and loss avoidance tend to take priority over making superior gains. And effective diversification is always employed to ensure that the risks of losses are limited as much as possible.

While real estate can be an effective method of diversification for the institutional investor, the average Singaporean does not have much in investment assets to make any hedges meaningful nor worthwhile. The primary residence is a residential property purchased for utility purposes. It is not an investment which can be sold to take advantage of market upturns and capital gains, or sold at the beginning of a market downturn to avoid losses. For other Singaporeans who own investment homes, their diversification is negligible if they have little in financial assets such as bonds and equities.

Fund managers managing large pools of money (in excess of hundreds of millions of dollars) and experienced portfolio managers also have access to expertise and resources to structure tax-efficient investment holding structures. They can also get access to legal, corporate secretarial, valuation and due diligence services at lower costs. Such expertise and professional services are normally not available to the retail investors since the advice and opinions would cost tens of thousands of dollars upfront, thereby reducing potential profits.

Again we need to highlight to readers that the correlation matrix is based on historical data, i.e. they are backward looking. The relationships between the asset classes change over time and should be monitored if they are used for balancing portfolios.

Even as any two asset classes demonstrate some correlation (either positively or negatively), it does not mean that a change in one asset class will directly cause a change to the other. Both asset classes are independent of each other, so although they may move in step with each other, the movement of one does not necessarily cause a movement in the other. For example, when both asset classes are trending up, it could be due to a rebound in the global economy. The statistical relationships shown in the correlation matrix do not provide any reasons why certain asset classes are good or bad hedges for other classes. While more complex methods and multivariate analysis (which we will not cover here) may be able to isolate and reveal the possible reasons for certain asset classes being a hedge for others, these analyses do not provide foolproof answers either. Most times, the answers are only valid within a limited range of parameters, assumptions and time periods under review. The answers from such analyses should not be extrapolated to future time periods as circumstances would have changed.

The average Singaporean investor with little access to all the data, and assumptions behind the data, may be treading blind as compared to investment banks and portfolio managers with good access to this data. And even when we do have the data, running the statistical analysis and executing on a 'hedging strategy' may not be practicable. The average Singaporean investor who has locked up most of his net worth in one or two residential properties can therefore hardly justify that he has a diversified investment portfolio and is hedged against the value-eroding impact of inflation.

Our conclusion

I spent more than two years to stew and re-stew this chapter. It is challenging to debunk long-held myths and even more challenging to demonstrate that a well-loved folklore DOES NOT exist.

We have spent far too much time trying to rack our brains pondering about why people believe that real estate and inflation indexes are somehow correlated. We believe that many people, especially the baby boomers, Gen X and Gen Y cohorts, have been repeating this unfounded tale so often that the folklore has become accepted as truth.

During the time researching, drafting and writing and re-writing this chapter, I was assisted by four brilliant university students: Joshua Toh Yi Xing, Brandan Koh Yee Swee, Joel Kam Jia Chuin and Dara Hanson. Their patience in researching and writing helped me to look at this issue with fresh eyes over and over.

This article has highlighted the fallacies with the problematic narrative we Singaporeans have attached ourselves to. It is ludicrous to assume that if inflation were constant and positive, then real estate prices will continue rising into perpetuity. Around the world, we have also seen instances where the relationship between inflation and housing prices is negative, such as when supply exceeds demand in European and Japanese cities with ageing populations.

Singapore's population is rapidly greying and the jobs-disrupted economy will mean a much slower population growth in future, if any. Rentals will drop as demand weakens and supply increases. Even then, inflation will march on at about 1-2% per annum. In such a scenario, how would real estate be a good and effective hedge against inflation?

Just as a rising tide will lift all ships, the statement "real estate is a hedge against inflation" is merely a manifestation of a growing economy lifting up inflation AND real estate prices at the same time. The recommendation to invest in real estate in order to hedge against inflation is a recommendation that stands on shaky grounds. At best, it is a concept used by institutional funds in their investments into investment grade assets rather than individual homes used by owner-occupiers.

Therefore, like many old wives' tales that we were told as kids, we recommend that this idea be banished altogether. However, I accept that readers' opinions will differ, just as I also accept that some people will always believe that Santa Claus exists.

23. | **Wealth Transfer with Real Estate**

Mr and Mrs Lim are about 65 years old and live in a 4-room flat with their second son who is a university student. Another son was recently married and moved out to his own HDB flat. Their flat is about 40 years old and recent transactions around the neighbourhood for similar flats show that its value is at or below $400,000.

Mrs Lim is holding a stable full-time job and has put in $170,000 of her CPF funds into the flat. Mr Lim was previously an odd-job worker, with negligible CPF monies. He contributed to the mortgage payments with cash. Both their cash savings are paltry but they managed to support their sons through university.

Although they have no more mortgage to pay, they are cognizant that the value of the flat has been declining slowly even though the neighbourhood was upgraded under the Home Improvement Programme (HIP) three years ago. The programme enhanced the neighbourhood's facilities, connectivity and common areas. But since the interiors of their flat is considered to be in "original condition", the value of their flat did not get a boost from the HIP.

Mr and Mrs Lim are considering between:

Option 1 – Staying put in this flat. But will they have enough cash for their retirement if they continued to live in this flat till they die?

Option 2 – Downgrading to a 3-room flat in the same HDB town so as to get more cash for a more comfortable retirement?

This story is very common amongst today's retirees and those approaching retirement. Many retired couples have one spouse who is a homemaker who has little in his/her CPF account while the other spouse is the long-term breadwinner who has some CPF that is generating a monthly pay out after he/she has turned 65.

If this story does not relate to you, perhaps you might think about your aged relatives who might be in, or approaching, the same situation. Then after reading this chapter, perhaps you might like to discuss with them their concerns about their retirement and their wishes for how their property or properties might be managed.

What this chapter is about

Discussing retirement and wealth transfer with real estate is rather complex. For most of us, the HDB flat we live in forms the largest fraction of our retirement "nest egg". We are a nation of asset-rich cash-poor people who have put most of our retirement funds, including CPF money, into the homes that shelter us.

I am not able to prescribe any solutions in this chapter. Instead, I will be asking many questions. Questions that are relevant for families to consider for their wealth transfer with real estate. The items that need to be discussed are similar whether the "real estate" is a single old 3-room flat or if the "real estate" consists of a portfolio of a dozen properties.

Circumstances differ for every single family and there are simply too many permutations for any simple, straightforward answer. However, going through the questions and considering as many potential eventualities as possible is a good thing.

Our list of questions can be classified along the 5 W's:

1. What – what is the property type, size, tenure and lease depreciation? What is the loan, if any, still attached to the property? Describe the property (asset versus liability) in detail.

2. Where – where are these properties? Where are the owners and beneficiaries? The locations of each party involved in the wealth transfer matters due to taxation.

3. Who – who are the named owners of the property or properties today? Who do you want to bequeath the property to? Are the beneficiaries qualified to own the property? If there are investment properties involved, who are the tenants, property managers, leasing agents, bankers and accountants related to these properties today? List down their contacts.

4. When – when do you want to transfer your property: while you are alive or after your demise? Will there be changes to tax treatments and ownership restrictions? When do you want different parts of your will to be executed?

5. Why – why are you doing this? why do you choose to do it this way? Why do you have to transfer your property to your beneficiaries instead of selling it and transferring cash to them? This final part serves as a check on your motivation and the pathway selected.

Back to Mr & Mrs Lim

A few pieces of data were offered for their consideration:

a. The life expectancy for residents at age 65 is about 21 years, so Mr and Mrs Lim would expect to live till 86.

b. According to a survey report titled "What older people need in Singapore: A household budgets study" published in May 2019, a dignified retirement lifestyle for single persons aged 65 and above would require a budget of $1,379 per month and for a couple aged 65 and above, a budget of $2,351 a month. This survey was led by renowned social services professors Ng Kok Hoe and Teo You Yenn.[1]

c. As HDB flats pass their 40-year mark, their values tend to depreciate faster. Please refer to Fig. 2 of Chapter 'F' on the estimated depreciation HDB value as the flats age beyond 40 years.

Based on the data above, for both options considered by Mr and Mrs Lim, either Mrs Lim or both of them will <u>need</u> to remain employed well into their 70s, or possibly into their 80s.

For Option 1, doing nothing means that the 4-room flat will continue to depreciate in value. Mrs Lim does not have much to collect from CPF as her CPF Retirement Account is far from the Minimum Sum target.

For Option 2, they could sell the 4-room flat and the proceeds of the sale will first be used to top up Mrs Lim's Retirement Account, and then they can purchase another 3-room flat. Assuming they sold the flat at $400,000, net of fees and selling expenses, and after topping up Mrs Lim's CPF with $110,000, they will have $280,000 of cash in the bank. A 3-room flat of the same 40 years age in their vicinity costs $300,000 and they can purchase one by using half of the money from the CPF Retirement Account (about $60,000) and part cash ($240,000). However, there are renovation costs and relocation costs to consider too. Taking this option will still mean that they have not much cash savings to support the next 20 years of living expenses. At least one of them will still need to stay employed.

---

1 https://whatsonough.sg/2019/05/22/what-older-people-need-in-singapore-a-household-budgets-study/

In the discussions with the Lim family, it seems that Mr and Mrs Lim are rather stuck on Option 2. They like the fact that the annual value decline of a 40-year-old 3-room flat will be much lower than their current 4-room flat. We offered other options for their consideration such as:

Option 3 – sell the flat and invest their money in low-risk government bonds, and then rent a 3-room flat ($1,700 a month) or rent a master-room ($1,000 a month) in a flat. But this arrangement, with cash savings invested and monthly pay outs from Mrs Lim's CPF, might only last them for about 10 years.

Option 4 – as they have both passed 65 years of age, they are eligible to sell down a part of their flat's 59 years of lease to HDB under the Lease Buy-back Scheme (LBS). For example, if they were to sell the tail-end 20 years of the 59 years lease, HDB might pay them, say $100,000 which will be used to top up both their CPF Retirement Accounts. Then each month, under the Retirement Sum Scheme (RSS), the CPF Board will pay Mr and Mrs Lim each several hundred dollars a month until the monies in their accounts dry up. This would mean that one of them would still need to seek employment as, according to the household budgets survey, the monthly budget for a couple requires about $2,350.

Option 5 – wait a few more years until their second son gets married and then buy a dual-key flat together with him. The sales proceeds of the 4-room flat will reduce the financial burden on the son's mortgage for the dual-key flat.

Each of these options have their shortfalls. It seems like Mr and Mrs Lim will have to survive on a monthly budget lower than the "budget for a dignified retirement" suggested in Prof Ng Kok Hoe's survey. Throughout the discussions we have always assumed that Mr and Mrs Lim are in good health and never considered medical expenses due to illnesses associated with old age. If medical expenses and other occasional recreational expenses were factored in, their current financial situation does not allow them to retire regardless which of the 5 options are selected. But what jobs and what salaries can they get at this age?

Moving forward

With more than 55,000 celebrating their 65th birthday each year for the next 40 years, there is an urgent need for families to think through their retirement adequacy, or for adult children to help their parents think through their parents' retirement adequacy. I will attempt to do more public education on this subject, reaching out to the retirees and their family members perhaps through Community Centres and online courses.

I have also teamed up with renowned Trust Specialist Mr Lee Chiwi from PreceptsGroup International to deliver courses on the subject of Wealth Transfer with Real Estate. Professionals in wealth management, front-line bankers, financial planners, wills writers, estate planners and real estate advisory specialists will need to be equipped with such knowledge to assist the hundreds of thousands of newly-retired families in the next decade. Our course will touch on the following:

a. Wealth transfer in the context typical of most Singaporean families where a large proportion of wealth is concentrated on real estate, particularly in their HDB flats.

b. Singapore's ageing demographics and the growing number of retirees and middle-class families which have HDB flats and condominiums as their main store of wealth.

c. Wealth transfer considerations related to HDB flats (and private residences), including the cash flow required to enjoy retirement, the depreciation of properties, dealing with outstanding mortgages, ownership restrictions, etc.

d. Potential issues around the transfer of properties and financial wealth when writing up a will and allocating the assets to beneficiaries.

This 1.5-day course will equip learners with the necessary knowledge to advise their clients and their families about the transfer of real estate holdings and financial assets to their loved ones. Finance professionals licensed by the Monetary Authority of Singapore could also qualify for monetary support from the Institute of Banking and Finance to get a 90-95% discount on the course fees.

Wrapping up

Today, 1 in 6 residents in Singapore are above 65. By 2030, 1 in 4 of us will be above 65. In absolute numbers, there will be a net increase of about 400,000 more residents above age 65 by the year 2030 as 600,000 will be crossing their 65th birthdays while 200,000 of those currently above 65 will be passing on.

Fig. 1: Population distribution by age cohorts in the year 2020.

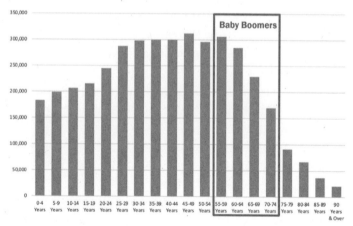

Source: Singstat, International Property Advisor

Most financial advisors simply assist their clients to plan their financial wealth. Be it retirement cash flow planning or inheritance and wealth transfer, most wealth managers do not consider the complexity of real estate assets. But as we can see from the case of Mr and Mrs Lim, even a modest 4-room HDB flat requires some planning and quite a lot of considerations.

There are many possible solutions and each family has its own preferences. There is no one-size-fits-all recommendation that I am able to give except to ask readers to think through the five W's with their families.

Then, having thought through the five W's and written down the details, regardless which path may be selected, it is advisable to get a will written and lodged with the Wills Registry that is maintained by the Singapore Academy of Law.

As parents, I am sure we would love to see our children and their children survive us happily. Let us not bequeath our homes in a mess for our children to fuss over after we are dead.

Postscript: For the research, interviews and analysis that went into this chapter and for producing associated presentation material, I am grateful for the contributions of Joel Kam Jia Chuin, Justin Chong Hou Shin and Victoria Chen Yun.

ABOUT THE AUTHOR

 Swee Yong is the CEO and the Key Executive Officer of International Property Advisor Pte Ltd. From Nov 2013 to Nov 2016, he was concurrently the CEO of Century 21 Singapore. Prior to running his own practice, he was a Director at the Real Estate Centre of Expertise at Société Générale Private Banking, responsible for advising clients on real estate investments, the Director of Marketing and Business Development at Savills Singapore and the General Manager at Far East Organization's Indonesia office.

He holds an MBA in Marketing from University of Hull, UK, and completed his BSc at the Imperial College, University of London, UK and the Institut Louis Pasteur, Université de Strasbourg, France.

Swee Yong's views are regularly featured in the *Straits Times, Business Times*, 新明日报, 联合早报, Channel NewsAsia, *TODAY*, StormAsia.com, etc. He has published 5 books on the property market: *Real Estate Riches, Building Your Real Estate Riches, Real Estate Realities, Weathering a Property Downturn* and *Preparing for a Property Upturn.*

He is one of very few property consultants who have been appointed as adjunct faculty at the Lee Kong Chian School of Business at the Singapore Management University (for both Master and Bachelor courses), at the Department of Real Estate in the National University of Singapore and at the School of Design and Environment at Ngee Ann Polytechnic.